MIDNIGHTS

JANE MILLER

DRAWINGS BY BEVERLY PEPPER

INTRODUCTION BY C.D. WRIGHT

ARTIST/POET COLLABORATION SERIES NUMBER **FOUR**

saturnalia books

ISBN: 978-0-9754990-6-1
Library of Congress Control Number: 2007925738

Saturnalia Books
13 E. Highland Ave.
2nd Floor
Philadelphia, PA 19118
info @ www.saturnaliabooks.com

Book Design by Saturnalia Books

Printing by Westcan Publishing Group, Canada

Distributed by:
UPNE
1 Court Street
Lebanon, NH 03766

Cover Art by Beverly Pepper (made with oil stick). Typeface is Helvetica Neue Ultralight manipulated with photoshop. The web drawings in the foldouts are made with lithograph sticks, pencil, ink, and charcoal. The colors have been desaturated. Full spread black work is oil stick and litho.

Jane Miller's Acknowledgments:

To my collaborator, the painter and sculptor Beverly Pepper, from whose high standards of work I hope I have not fallen too far, my deepest gratitude.

To my reader, the poet Barbara Cully, friend, thank you for the hours.

To my editor, Henry Israeli, thank you for the freedom to compose.

To poet C.D. Wright, for introducing this book — there aren't better words than her own with which to thank her: "I wish I had known more of your company."

To Penny Cooper and Rena Rosenwasser, for their unflappable good spirits, immeasurable generosities, and a home in the hills and in their hearts, my humble thanks.

To my longtime friends, my love, for making yourselves fully present, often well past midnight.

My appreciation to the editors of the following publications, in which some of these works appeared:

The American Poetry Review, Pool (interview conducted by Stephanie Brown); *Colorado Review* (in a slightly different version).

OTHER BOOKS BY JANE MILLER

A PALACE OF PEARLS

WHEREVER YOU LAY YOUR HEAD

MEMORY AT THESE SPEEDS: NEW AND SELECTED POEMS

AUGUST ZERO

WORKING TIME: ESSAYS ON POETRY, CULTURE AND TRAVEL

AMERICAN ODALISQUE

BLACK HOLES, BLACK STOCKINGS (CO-AUTHOR, OLGA BROUMAS)

THE GREATER LEISURES

MANY JUNIPERS, HEARTBEATS

Introduction by C.D. Wright

Poetry is nothing if not equipped for crisis. Sharp and penetrating, it cuts through every fear by which we are secretly governed; brings them to the light of the page and names them. Total exposure. Anything less is not an option, not if "[you] want to live in the world in [your] right mind." The poet does. Even so, the lovers will part, the mother begin to die. Losses, Gentle Reader, will mount.

This takes many midnights. Many crossings. By car (listening to someone else's music); by air (listening to the same track over and over). Beds are "glistened in" in ugly motels, in guest houses; under skylights in foreign cities. Friends enlisted: a filmmaker, a yogi, a Russian princess disguised as gardener, art patrons, glass-blowers, writers and painters past and present. Friends offer the best intervention. They are there for you, and likewise, you, when you were not the one suffering, have seen their most vulnerable parts exposed, flapping in the unflinching sun-shine. The filmmaker's backstory is lit up and her sister and cousin are catapulted out of a truck, just like that, blown to their premature graves.

The poet's mother begins to die. The daughter attends. A brother arrives on his wings. A cousin glides in and out with a dancing partner. The dancing partner's backstory is lit up and exposed, including terrible places where children are held when their relatives get deported. Chinese prescriptions are taken on a schedule. A French rosé is ruefully added to the mix. The *I Ching* is consulted. The beach heaves into view.

The border between Mexico and the U.S. is crossed. A migrant's face is sheared off by a vigilante. Actual, undocumented workers are passed digging actual holes. The Holocaust is recalled. A slice of the Führer's insane plan is decreed. The poet Celan is lost to us all over again. The lovers, in Amsterdam, walk through the Anne Frank Huis weeping. At some point, the dry winds of the Gobi bring the whole shoot to a stand-still. For months on end.

Lovers part (almost by definition). Desire can never complete the mission to close with the lover once and forever. Failure fuels it. "Desire, as the yogi teaches, does not lead to contentment."

Movies, paintings, and books stream through the poet's memory vault. They are called in "not [to] confuse reality but illumine it." Perhaps to contribute a few cues — how to live, how to endure. Poetry's privileged perch is not stable. "Poetry is speech by someone who is in trouble," is one poet's definition. Experience need not be assimilated. Art need not be separated. The poet would bid Virginia Woolf rise out of the Ouse emptying the stones from her pockets. She would that artists endure.

Jasmine, lavender, blended vintages, a spray of fine perfume, Camembert cheese, big pink California roses overflow the set. Wherever Jane Miller goes the senses will gather.

The goal is not to make sense of, but art of this story. The goal is not to make a story but to experience the whole mess. There are mental sufferings and physical sufferings to go through; to apprehend if one can. There are the spent casings of history to sift through, pick up and examine. Calm-like, hysterical, forensic. This life not just a worn passage.

In Beverly Pepper's formidable drawings "it is mostly midnight / inhabiting a strange place." Black columns thrust upward but are stobbed short of the paper's edge. Their exterior walls are roughed up. An open structure is shown in hatchings and planes, accompanied by a dense sheaf of lines. A pair of unmatched bottles, a fish, and a triangle, erotically slit, are inferred, but mostly it is midnight. The light structures the black field, else stripes it, else momentarily flashes through the darkest areas. The text is fortified, even ennobled by their presence though the drawings resist standing as sentinels; they resist giving shelter. Their overall tonic effect serves the book better than consolation, however intensely the nights are discharged.

Herein, Jane Miller applies her considerable lyric stamina to the paragraph. Not a journal, not a narrative — *these outpourings* she says at one point, but they are much more formal and fetching than the word conveys. *Pure crying*, she says, but the tears come in shifts and are dried by sustained commentary on their source, even their comparative insignificance, yet individuated as they must be. Four discrete lyrics are in position to wick off any excess in the prose.

The mother soils herself and the daughter bathes her with a warm washcloth. The lover leaves and the poet pukes a divine meal in a divine hotel room. Don't empty your suitcase yet, Gentle Reader—there's a funeral, a two-stringed instrument with the scroll of a horse's head, a brief treatise on owls, a little subversive music to foil the junta—whole new pathways articulating their coursings to and from the heart until the last syllable sings itself out.

"Preparation is all. Attention is required." What a splendid testament to the ill fortunes of love.

The beauty of the world, which is so soon to perish, has two edges, one of laughter, one of anguish, cutting the heart asunder.

— Virginia Woolf, *A Room of One's Own*

LOST NIGHT

It is mostly midnight
      inhabiting a strange space.
           It makes no difference to me

it's three in the afternoon
      at one of many stopping places,
           the height of summer.

There isn't a breath.
      The air is stony, the stone walls dusty,
           the dust still, gritty, sandy;

the sand too hot. Several women in black clothes
      shell peas on short stools
           sitting tight to a white wall

for forty years. Bleary-eyed fishermen
      knit the tears in their nets. A child's eyes
           shine at the door, two small animals fearing

the visitors, who are screwing up their lives
      slowly, on holiday, *why did you say that?*
           And then more quickly, once home,

you don't know me,
      beyond therapy, beyond boundaries, *please stay,*
           I beg you; get out.

You go far. It feels like I am going
      blind, I leave the desert for the coast with a friend
           who takes pity on me

the way you take liberties.
           You acquiesced? That shall always remain
           a mystery. You go where?

Crete, memory / border crossing, Arizona – California, 3 p.m.

1

i

Those who make it north across the border to Tucson have considered what are power and slavery. Those of us asleep can only dream we are running, thirsty, scared, and wounded, through a forest of stinging cacti, with helicopters spraying light like an automatic garden sprinkler, an automatic weapon spraying death, which keeps coming round to little blue violets expiring of thirst, dying of exposure. It takes more than a broken poet,

more than the most sacred heart, more than a cathedral to hold them in its embrace, these women and girls and boys and men being fired upon. Those of us who are writers write about the forlorn. They are not we in any case.

Yet, we are all mixed up in this test of love, order, disorder, and dishonor. What is your secret? Your shame? Your guilt? Your thrill, at whose expense? Jew, neither your shaved head because you are enslaved, nor your shaved head because, by your own people, you are betrayed, makes us all Jews.

There is the line, *What difference would one day make?*, which appears in the film *Head in the Clouds*, about an irresistible woman who appears to be collaborating with the Nazis during World War II,

except she is really in the French underground. Unfortunately, one of the good citizens of her village slits her with a knife before the villagers find out, the next day, that she was one of them. Even after learning the truth, her murderer still felt in his heart that she betrayed his sister to save others, sacrificed his sister, in effect; his guilt is not simple, not black and white. Nor is hers; the actor playing the Nazi officer's mistress spoke courageously in an interview about guilt, responsibility, and justice. The conversation dwindled, and she added, minorly, "Unfortunately, we shot a scene at Sacré-Cœur on our last night [that] didn't make the film, which was really sad. But it was just incredible to have that entire church closed down. It was two in the morning and [we were] just kind of watching the view and shooting the scene."

I admire that Charlize Theron indulges in a private thought on beauty, hours after midnight, and shares it with a stranger, an interviewer, a writer trying to capture an intimate reflection. Notwithstanding, the film, of course, is as important as the actor, because, through her, the film represents insanity beyond designated border, long past midnight,

metaphorically, in the life of the twentieth century. This one dead sister, a subplot really, of the film, is dead, by mistake? Bad luck? A choice? A sacrifice? Neither philosopher nor historian, I can only be returned, by the film, closer to home, to ask a Mexican who wants to be American,

an American Mexican, a Mexican who works in America, an American American, who vacations in Mexico, like a Russian American, an Italian American, or possibly a Jewish American (i.e., special religious American category, as in Arab American, not a country of ancestry but an ancestry of spirit, as when referring to Mexico as Catholic, or indigenous, or rebellious, or revolutionary). Who answers for the dead sister caught in a crossfire? My nightmare as a writer

is that I will have to say something. Yes, I must speak for the sister. Please, she is dead. Her death saved others. A martyr. Is it clear why she dies? Her brother would like to know, please, what happened, to blame whom? First, he makes a choice; he knows whom to blame. Then, he feels how? I would like to hold him in my arms.

The dead are becoming dead at the Mexican border because, in their case, they are not someone's sisters who became exposed passing information meant to save a dozen lives. They are moving their own bodies, one at a time, through a desert with armed helicopters hovering thirty yards above the pricked earth. A wall is being built to make crossing the border harder. I have failed to leave plastic water bottles in designated places for the crossing. Nor, I confess, can I get a man who slit a woman's throat, in revenge, to understand death. I cannot correct death, nor take down so much as an emotional wall without a pill and a glass of treated water. I can only make a safe drive across an unprotected border into Arizona from California, lost in thought, *Head in the Clouds*. (I watch movies, I read books. Therefore, what?) Therefore Reality? Where is it?

There's the Seine, seen in the far distance from one of the world's great cathedrals at the head of Montmartre. I want to live in the world in my right mind. And here is one survivor, without a lesson in mind, with the walls of his religion completely detonated, the cathedral of his family completely detonated, and the view from a great mind completely detonated. Here is poet Paul Celan, and he jumps into the moving river.

In his pocket calendar he has written, "Depart Paul."

Sonoran Desert / Paris, Sacre-Cœur, 2 a.m.

Hours of metaphor ought not confuse reality but illumine it. One night cracked me — as though someone had taken a chainsaw down the center of our bed lengthwise, and also to my head. That night's cleaving was as unexpected as nature's, and less kind, if one takes the measure of the moon every month, reduced gradually, gracefully, amidst clouds, stars, or alone. When you said you were going ahead with plans I'd begged you to cancel, both of us recognized our increasingly labyrinthian course had becalmed. It was stormy; I was screaming my head off, what was left of it.

I do not regret sitting on my feet, and, as upright as possible under the bombardment of language, begging you. (I try to hold this position each morning, with my silent partner, wind, to strengthen my spine and my heart *chakra*.) Through watery eyes, I saw you venture into a watery stream of lies. Your brown eyes got darker and drier the more unmoored from you I became, until I could only say, let us go to the airport right now, and do the trip together. Tell her the golden thread attached around her, like a dog — she's unleashed. Tell her you are staying with me, going with me.

No, I am determined, you said, and I thought, when one loses one thing, there can be a spell on her and she can lose everything. And you let fly, first, words at me, then, yourself into the night sky to another continent. Night fell, appropriately, into what is only the next day, the unknown. I sat on this edge once as a younger woman, on the windowsill of my grandmother's kitchen, long after she had children, daughters, and the daughters had daughters and sons. Some dead and some living of this group gathered at her house, at various times, for holiday. By this time, she was dead, and we were bound by ties that held us entire, as in puppetry, should anyone fall and fail to catch onto something.

I leaned from the ledge and saw the loveliest hanging flowers, which were not dangling from a neighbor's pot on an upper floor of the apartment building, as reality would bear, but rather from higher, much higher I know because I leaned to see, nearly losing my balance. Barbara, my cousin, dead of breast cancer, pulled me back not with a translucent hand but with her voice, and not with words but with laughter, pleasure, at seeing the flowers she painted swaying in front of our grandmother's window. The colorful purple nightshade confirmed that I was dreaming. Nightshades live on earth, in earth. They do not dangle like paper sculpture on barely visible threads from a ceiling nor from a celestial body.

Nightshade is your favorite color, purple, with its complement, yellow, but people are not as accepting of their reality as nature is. We would not survive as a couple. You got promptly on a jet with someone else. It came to light,

and now I sleep on my sawed half of the bed, clinging to the saw-toothed, uneven tear. Consciousness is my bedfellow. Lovers, we are aware of the third dimension, space, where opposition dissolves and triangulates, and of the fourth, the time a fine line artfully estranges one's creation.

Tucson, midnight and beyond

6

I insist we unload everything. Victoria is patient with me, although she feels strongly that if one feels one shall not be robbed, one shall not. Impressively, her soul extends into her thinking. Nevertheless, I make her unload the car, and the motel manager hauls the heavy bags up to the second floor into the dark, spacious, ugly room. We have driven six hundred miles, mostly through desert, listening to Victoria's 1980s disco and 1990s Latin music compilations. We immediately hook into a TV show on the history of AIDS, its various incarnations among monkeys in Africa, among bathhouse participants in San Francisco, among heterosexuals with ripped condoms, among addicts sharing needles. Next, the whole fucking mess with the drug companies unwilling to lower their prices, and the government not allowing enough of the dying to experiment with drugs not officially approved.

We are riveted to the set, with the olive curtains drawn tight against the freeway. Victoria has driven most of the day because of my situation. Instead of going to the International House of Pancakes, which we save for breakfast, I suggest we dine on peanut butter and wheat crackers. She refuses, but gets hungry and eats. I take a bath, the last one I take for a week. Why? This happens and then that happens.

To you, Victoria, a filmmaker and writer, making the choice of these words all the more grave and essential, I would like to say that what little I know of love (that I declared nevertheless wholeheartedly to my lover) has been dimensionalized by you a thousand-fold, folds like fans that open and become a form of beauty, Japanese origami, say, or a wild rose captured in time-lapse photography. Or, more commonly in the history of art, there is the image of a nude woman, which opens and opens to interpretation, yielding thousands of gazes that disturb her, and still she remains essentially, inexhaustibly lovely. Love, you have shown me, is about something, an action, an organizing principle, an ethic, a being, not a general idea.

After the AIDS victims have completely broken us, and we are plastic molded dolls whose legs and arms lie detached from our torsos, it's impossible to arrive at our destination before we are repaired by dream. We sleep in strange beds, where thousands have folded into themselves, waking unobserved and lovely, or unlovely, conditioned by cold air along an American freeway.

Best Western, Buttonwillow, California, midnight

Victoria's little sister disappeared from earth many years ago. Soon, we will be able to view what happened to her when she hurtled out the back of a pick-up. Their cousin's body, also, god help us, flew out of its soul. These are kids with given names, Christians who were baptized — Victoria, now living in L.A., making films, Virginia dead, and also the cousin. I cannot remember her name. I cannot make up her name. One needs to understand the turpitude in changing the true names for the sake of art; however poorly, and from whatever weakened heart art emerges, that dread must not befall it.

One could think of a hundred names for the cousin, especially lovely in Spanish, because of the vowel at the end, like a cello note concluding. And still, she shall remain… (but what is her name? I cannot remember).

Virginia and this younger cousin set out on a ride that ends badly. My father Walter keeps being denatured by cancer, and Brien's father pulls the fucking trigger over and over. What happens next, in our minds, what? If reality is subjective, why don't they come back to life? (The experience of reality is subjective.)

There are tigers crouching above and tigers crouching below, until they turn into jasmine, and my mind cannot imagine anything more auspicious. Unfortunately, I can barely imagine that many tigers still roam the earth, but I feel, in my tired heart, two girls (ages eight and six) redolent of jasmine, roaming the earth, as surely as the sun roams the sky, and the moon behind the sun. The girls roam as celestial bodies, without desire, and, as wise Mirto proposes, everyone deserves to be desired, so the situation is dire.

Victoria is not trying to make sense, but, rather, to make art, of this story, which I tell haltingly, and can only, by low comparisons, bring close to home. When somebody suggests that I shadow someone, so as not to be alone with loneliness or madness crouching nearby, does she include someone dead? Kim, my darling, children are dead all over again, that much is certain, as your grandmother is like unto dead, frail, losing her mind, cackling like the insane, falling down, dehydrated, a figure in a dream except that, as Lorca said, *No es un sueño la vida. ¡Cuidado! ¡Cuidado! ¡Cuidado! (Life is not a dream. Careful! Careful! Careful!)* If MaMa remembers to turn off the gas burner, it is a good day. If she can sort one pill from another, and not take all at once, it is a good day. If your PaPa wants, and gets, chocolate before he fails the inhalation of his last breath, it is a good day.

A mind cannot fathom a situation more dire and more propitious than the loss of these two children, over and over, for Victoria, nor the loss of these grandparents, for you, my beloved, to whom I am now not speaking, not even a religious mind can fathom for you two sufferers anything worse, not even the Honorable, His Holiness, the Dalai Lama, who must shadow a billion Chinese.

There is a story, in which one's mind and spirit, if they are not thrown from a vehicle, conspire to anoint our lips with lipstick and choose onto whom they smear it. Desire prepares our clean chins to trickle dark wine down them. Sometimes, false desire enters a translucent, organza gown and high heels for a long evening of dancing under the roaming moon, and a drive home under the roaming sun. The morning is already boiling. The open convertible takes to the dirt highway. This is someone or other coming home from the prom. The assignation is with the wrong date, the wrong time.

Analogically, it is at the right time and the right place that we die.

The children die of internal bleeding and the children are dead. Victoria, as a young girl, changes her mind at the last minute about getting into the truck for the festivities. Two angels, living in Texas, get thrown like meat onto counters. If the Dalai Lama has any reason to shadow me, which he does not — why would a specialist in the dismantling and reconstructing of the finest timepieces waste his time here? — would His Highness ever forgive me for the metaphors I fall prey to? How I hide behind words like an extinct being? But if, Highness, I may have a moment of your time, I might inquire, Must one back the imagination out from incursions that alter reality? Do such excursions end in dishonor? Holiness, I believe in art, but it goes missing. Reality must be changed, imaginatively, yes? One must reread Coleridge? and learn of fancy v. truth, and one must read Einstein, and learn of paradox, and, Holiness, before the bell rings... but the bell is ringing.

Victoria's movie will show a simple summer afternoon without shadow. This is the other reason she drives all over Los Angeles, day and night: not only is she looking for her missing sister, she is looking for money to make her movie. Victoria roams the city of Los Angeles, driving too fast on the freeway and closing too close when cars suddenly halt. Caroline's not acting when she shrieks, *Stop*. Otherwise, she is. Remember, this is Hollywood. Everybody's got to make a living.

cruising Sunset Strip, late

10

v

After I told my mother that my relationship had ended, and I was shaken, shaking, she got nervous and lost weight, as she had around the time I was born. Which accounts for her being photographed in a chinchilla stole and gold lamé dress on a cure at the Fontainebleau in Miami Beach around 1950 in front of palm trees on wallpaper inside the lobby. She looks like she has put on the pretty dress without removing its hanger, and a little wind inside her is making it shimmer.

Victoria has recently deposited me high in the Berkeley hills into an empty house, a fact that suited my mood entirely, either positively or negatively, depending on my mood, and depending on the hour I took a particular prescription. Medicine, which I myself suggested to my mother's doctor to help her, and which, subsequently, sent her to the emergency room.

Victoria, who pulls the empty space into a living space despite my continuing to feel that I am in a bubble of a car, an incubator, or the inside of a closed rose, does not prefer to wake at 4 a.m. Victoria, who, after all, is an excellent driver, could very well drive one of the medical ambulances which transport trained individuals into homes to save lives when daughters cannot hear increasing cries for help from their mothers. It is not, however, on her agenda to pause from a dream to drive such a daughter to such and such an airport to catch up with an ambulance in Sunrise.

The daughter is alive in the past, as midnight turns into the earliest morning hours, against whose darkness stars are brightest. What year is it, Kim? Are we still in the same bed? Am I dreaming of the moon above an open-air station? ...the last light in a claustrophobic station? Our bed is in a bowl of mountains. You want to know, Are those sirens? an ambulance? What suspect is loose? Has somebody crossed? We stiffen with fear, our journey interrupted. It is only New Year's Eve, I am trying to tell you, only fireworks, only celebration. Go back to sleep... May I have the rest of the night back again? I would like to sit up and listen to the spells that follow... But I'm called elsewhere, years later, and it is by an ambulance this time, and it is to my mother's home for the time being.

I get out of the car. It is not the one Victoria has magnanimously driven me to Berkeley in, because our battery has died the day before. That car had to be towed specifically to Concord, California, being under a special warranty, which peoples' bodies deserve. I recognize neither this car, nor poor Victoria, asleep, and yet not asleep between worlds, and am caught by surprise when the airport's glass doors automatically part.

I was just beginning to infer something from doors opening suddenly and closing dispassionately and determinedly behind one. And again, to open and to close, over and over, without prejudice, to travelers, regardless of circumstance, creed, race, mental state, or marital status. I acknowledge the general visage of destiny — the airport looked like it was on the same prescription I was on, tranquilized in the wrong hue, a green not in literature but in medical literature.

Oakland Airport, 5 a.m.

I land in Florida the way some people land up in Florida; that is, I feel I will never leave. I administer a pill to myself, and a shaving of a pill to mother when we settle in, after she returns from her overdose. Either mother or I wake crying, and are attended by the other. This fails one midnight when mother wakes with low groans, dropping blood pressure, and shitting her bed and herself. I clean her up.

The essence of the moment is in having the washcloth the exact temperature of the warm sea of summer. I change the bedding, but her death commences again. Then she says what my father said to her the night he died, *Do whatever you want with me.* One of his arms manages to pull her head down to his hospital bed so he can kiss her (goodbye). The story of their last kiss has become a private poem; it emerges as life necessitates. The inchoate language of the poem tonight rouses me to make frantic phone calls as mother begins to look like a translucent eggshell, and sees back to where she was born, moaning beyond me.

I've heard other people describe this moment, these mid-nights, involving one's mother's soft body and an old washcloth. I can only say that this is the most beautifully configured, thirty-odd thousandth washed, and only, ninety-year-old body I have ever seen. Her mind is going in one way, mine another. Yet, we visit the same states of fear and resolve, and we endure our moment of grandeur together; it is grand because it is endured. Together. By phone, my sister-in-law advises me, in a sharp tone, which I receive dramatically slowed, to call the medics now. When they arrive, they are loathe to take Flossie to the emergency room again, until they take her pressure and it is eighty over forty, at which point the larger medic tears open mother's second nightgown of the night and flings her bones onto a stretcher. I beg to be allowed to go with her on the exact stretcher. Next, I lose myself by locking onto the eyes of the other medic, molded and beautiful, as if she has been hand-blown and fired and cooled. I awake for one infrared second out of a grave, where I have let myself fall over my mother's body, having failed to clothe and wash and attend her, only to be immediately buried again with shortness of breath, shaking, etc. I still see this serious young woman now as if I have opened the kiln — Jesus, where is my head? — where she was placed burning, and then the door slams at the back of the ambulance. Nothing can be saved by writing. Nor anyone. It's a complete waste of time. One is simply preparing oneself, perhaps by writing, to be capable of driving to an emergency room and lying on the floor next to her (the medic? the mother?) most of the night. That part of night that is very early morning, as everyone knows and no one says.

The doctor on call does nothing because her pressure has stabilized, and because he is fighting to save two bulging men from heart attacks. They both die. I watch from my womb position on the floor, out mother's open door, to the open door of the failed defibrillations, and I watch the solemn, fiercely exhausted warriors file out of their failures, and continue their rounds. I watch the doctor type up the reports, Dead: so and so. Dead: so and so, much as I am typing this now.

When I take her home, I call a doctor, who calls a doctor who will admit her to a mental facility to calm her anxiety and regulate her blood pressure. Things which once had layers of ambiguity now seem egregiously literal. The Pavilion is locked.

At each door, visitors are treated to a circumlocution of their bodies by a nurse wielding a metal rod that picks up potentially harmful objects forbidden to patients. There never appear to be any transgressions. Mother's shower cap was taken from her when she checked in, as was her comb.

When my brother flies from Düsseldorf, Germany, to New York, to Florida to join us, I help him fold his wings and check them in the cloakroom. Our cousin Barbara, called hurriedly, arrives straight from her dancing class in the glass slippers of a fairytale, which, for her, began with a controlling father who disallowed dancing. Through the glass slippers, I see the scars formed by her running away from home over and over. Now we are adults; now we are all being scanned by the metal rod, now we are being admitted to the unit. Why Düsseldorf, what my brother was doing there, briefly becomes the topic of conversation, which never has an answer, there might as well not be a Düsseldorf, and for mother and for me there never will be.

Finally there is our mother, in a white sweater with pink roses so lovely someone will no doubt steal it, which would be a crime of the heart since her skeleton looks nearly elegant in it. You who are given the task of the daily dissemination of meds at exactly 11 a.m. and at bedtime, for god's sake, if you want the hand-knit sweater, enjoy it for the rest of your life, because here we are locked and guarded, here we are metal-detected, safe, freed from our tears by you. But please, tell us, without our Düsseldorf, where are we?

The Pavilion, special visiting hours, bedtime

vii

Mother remains behind glass in The Pavilion. My brother and I invite our cousin Barbara to dinner. Pedro Aguilar accompanies her. Pedro Aguilar's life is movement. He is her dancing partner. Pedro lives in the world as glass that is formed and reformed, shaped by heat. He is always being reborn, unlike my brother and I, whose glass has hardened into a shield, which makes us protect ourselves from death, rather than live.

When they are children, the court removes Pedro, his brother Antonio, and his sister Socorro from relatives who are in this country without papers, ordering them to the Mount Loretta Orphanage. Next, they are placed in foster care. (Care foster in placed are they next.) He takes his siblings from foster care and makes it to Sister Cathy at the Foundling Hospital headquarters to tell her of their being locked in a room on weekends, and about being physically abused. (Abused physically, locked in a room, abused in a room, on weekends locked in a room, physically, on weekends, physically locked, Sister Cathy.)

In return, the state separates the children into other foster homes. Rather than press two palms against the glass window, he takes his dancing partners in his hands; Pedro Aguilar asks for his siblings' addresses to write them, and retrieves them, in the city that treats them as premature babies who are not to be touched. What a hospital we stick figures inhabit, with our noses pressed to glass! Pressed to glass, we are left to think of our lovelies, Are they dead? Are they moving? Pedro moves through glass without it shattering. He will not live in a hospital. He will live in a dance hall. He will live *en clave* — a five-note pattern that serves salsa music.

Beginners learn to identify *clave* and apply it to certain spins. (I cannot hear in the incubator, I cannot see.) Advanced beginners learn to hear *clave* and apply it to basic mambo and salsa patterns (In a relationship, the role of "object of desire" must be exchanged from time to time.) Intermediate and advanced dancers add syncopation, styling, shines, patterns, and turns. (Couples are destined for one another and destined to oppose one another.) And at the master mambo level, the dancer incorporates distinctive body and hand movements. (Do not touch me ever again.)

Cousin Barbara (the one still living, of two cousins with the same name) and Pedro, who is always alive, are right now in the grand ballroom styling, spinning, shining, patterning, and turning, without counting, to the celestial rumba. My brother and I cannot see or hear them, enthralled by our reflections.

Finally, the crystal lights in the ballroom dim and the dancing shadows, out of step, cling awkwardly. The first stone is thrown. We cowards are not alone; there is a world of cowards. The glass partitions shatter, and the ballroom crystals fall. And there are Barbara and Pedro, styling, spinning, shining, patterning, and turning, turning, flattening the crushed glass until it is a smooth surface. They step lightly out from here into thin air.

Gold Coast Ballroom, Coconut Creek, Florida, 11 p.m.

viii

I return. Something continues. I must try to live like the giants I admire, who could not live — Paul Celan, Virginia Woolf — but who anyway lived, suffering mind bends. They were like divers who lost the frame of mind to remember, in time, to decompress before surfacing. Although I'm drawn to water, I am without the courage to die; seasick and sea-driven,

I am driving from Berkeley to the beach with a yogi and a glassblower, winding, slowing, breathing, opening the windows for the redwood scent, for the eucalyptus, for fog. Fewer and fewer houses, fewer and fewer businesses, curves, a country store, a post office, a market, a bakery. Then, more slow turns. The yogi is breathing evenly next to me. And behind, the glassblower, breathing into her invisible, flexible, heated glass. The yogi puts her legs behind her head; the glassblower blows three glass bubbles and juggles them in the backseat, with her eyes closed. Now the yogi's eyes also are closed, as she practices her art. We arrive at the ocean, itself tremendously, unconditionally, matrimonially, impartially, indifferently, and, consciously or not, breathing in and out of the shoreline's mouth.

The yogi and the glassblower spring out of the car toward the beach. They let me spend hours watching them breathe on a blanket. The glassblower spills sand through her fingers, like an hourglass that cares neither what time it is, nor what time is. The yogi lies on her belly and buries her feet and covers her head with a scarf. She's headless. Yet, she has mastered breathing. She fills her lungs to capacity; I imagine she could hold her breath crossing the Pacific to the Hawaiian

Islands, not that she would. Her practice is breathing, not not breathing. The things I don't know about her could fill the ocean as far as I can see. Right now I'm limited to seeing if I can breathe.

For one who is breathing shallowly, the valiant autonomic nervous system, ruled by chaos, regretfully or not, pulls in the next breath. We hope. And this is our blessing, our curse: we ought to be aware of our breathing, of when we stop, but instead we hope to be breathing. I watch the yogi and the glassblower laugh, shyly telling the story of how they fell in love, slowing, winding the curves of first seeing one another at a party, and then again, somewhere, and then, fewer and fewer houses, fewer and fewer people, more and more scented air, and then, their first kiss, which takes even a poor, inexperienced breather to a resting place.

The afternoon continues. They talk, nap, meditate. One is an invisible bubble and the other is a lion, a tiger, a dog. Each speaks of having died for love and returned as a dog, as a lion, as a collection of colorful globes. Now I know I will have to get up from our blanket and walk and walk, more and farther, until I get to where I left my father Walter when he died. For this is the beach I visited and visited from the house Kim and I had nearby, out of breath and out of a father, when he died thousands of miles from here, where I had to leave him. There he is. As invisible, as dead, as bald and smiling, as light blue-eyed as ever. Hello I say, opening wide on the *o*.

My elderly mother glides through the *o* of my mouth, as matter-of-factly as she let herself out the door of The Pavilion, normally locked to mental patients, as she has convinced the good doctor to release her to her family. My brother takes her to New York, and I take her inside me, standing on her head and breathing deftly into a glass bowl, to the near end of this long beach. I hear her say, explicitly, I hope you are well, I cannot take care of you; I am trying to take care of myself.

Here is Flossie, discharged like a very slow moving bullet backward; here is her husband, my father. Here I am, crying into a yogi who has made of herself a transparent glass to collect my tears, and my brother is back in New York. I say to you frankly now that if you are breathing shallowly, because you know in your heart, where everything hurts, that you are scared to death, no, scared of death, that you are fine, or you will find that you are fine, and then you will die.

Point Reyes National Seashore, all afternoon

First Night Under Water

After a gargantuan
        meal mid-day, we hit the street
                with barely anything to say.

I get the guy whose storefront
        ceramics you admire
                down from his apartment

in his undershirt. He sells us
        a dozen saucers and cups
and an extra set thrown in for luck

we're going to need, driving back
to our grand hotel,
                the full moon
chasing along your side most of the way.
I understand its meaning
                as a moment

of nostalgia, until God takes a poison
        arrow to it and its guts spill out, o'er-flooding
                your flask of tequila,
which I ought to replace with gasoline for you

to accelerate in hell
        in heat, my phantasmagoric cat.

You are compelled to ask
                if we are there yet.
The answer is enflamed language.
        Then our first night under water

darkens the stain
        of your wine-drenched evening gown.
Yes, my love, drown.

Umbria, Italy, timeless

ix

Wise Mirto suggests I retell Kim the Fassbinder movie about Maria Braun. Mirto is enough of a fool to suffer fools like me once a week. A very clever fool, she empties herself, takes in the human drama, then empties again. I hope on her own time she is filling with the nectar of the gods and enjoying an evening of slow drinking, an evening of being slowly drunk, an evening of being. Today she has reminded me about Maria Braun.

As I remember it, a couple falls in love, gets caught up in an explosion at the marriage registrar, a scene which is confusing and nearly slapstick, and they don't get to consummate their marriage; they become separated by circumstances of history and destiny. The husband, I think, gets sent to the Russian front. In any case, Maria Braun is forced to fend for herself. By any number of shrewd and demeaning acts, she uses her great beauty and guile to conquer political and business worlds and become a corporate success, a woman of tremendous means, while remaining loyal to her lover, except for a slip-up or two in a necessary or uncontrollable moment. Perhaps her lover is in jail for some petty or serious crime. Perhaps he has murdered someone, or been accused of murder unjustly, or perhaps he is off supporting his mother as an ironworker, or or or. I simply can't remember.

I do know that memory itself has a telltale function in Fassbinder's archetypal tale, a project which, among other causes, e.g., incessant work, incessant smoking, sleeplessness, excessive sex, or excessive lack of sex, I can't remember; poor diet, drug overdose, etc., kills him at thirty-seven, my lover's age when she's readying herself to leave. Mirto suggests I retell Kim *The Marriage of Maria Braun*.

Students of German history know well the story, as do feminists, acolytes of Fassbinder the artist, patrons of art houses, most Germans, married couples possessed by material objects, psychologists investigating power, homosexuals obsessed with the filmmaker's personal histrionics, admirers of epic comedy and romantic ballad, therapists excavating remnants of the unconscious by utilizing analogy, etc.

Maria's lover, as is well known, returns from war, exile, jail, his mother, ironworking, or whatever, to Maria and her vast fortune and huge estate, and promptly feels outclassed. He leaves for what turns into many more years, during which time he accrues a gigantic fortune, a sum greater even than our single-minded Maria has accrued by squeezing competitors' testicles with pincers so that, by comparison, her lover's passion will be incomparable.

Their reunion is brief. In the fairytale, he returns in an elegant suit with an elegant briefcase, they have coffee, and he goes upstairs to shower. Maria follows. We do not see, but we know, that they make love on fine Egyptian linens, each coming a couple of times, exploding with laughter and pain. Maria returns to the kitchen for a well-deserved cigarette. She has taken to smoking with cigarette holders, as I recall, of ebony. She turns on the gas stove and leans close, as one might lean for the first sip of Billecart-Salmon, after being reunited with one's soul mate, whom she believed she would never see or touch again.

Maria is not in the same world as Fassbinder, who may have just had a blowjob, or wants one desperately, is totally coked up, has forgotten his medication for days, is dehydrated, and probably hasn't showered. We are attracted and repulsed, not by him really (after all, he is only Fassbinder), but by his characters (because they are you and I). Fassbinder is involved in technical activity, and therefore is aware, as we are not, that Maria neglected to turn off the gas when she made coffee earlier. When she lights the match, the mansion, the power couple, the German work ethic, and the movie screen blow up like a suicide's head.

Why tell my love? To avoid a ten-year separation that could empower her emotionally and financially, having read me (incorrectly) as more achieved? To invite a ten-year separation as a means of coming to learn how much we miss, and therefore, love, and are destined for one another? To understand grief that persists and deepens may signal a return of passion? To take back every insecure pincer's bite I inflicted on her polished arguments, such that ten years is like unto ten seconds, or a tenth of a second, and she is here lying on a blanket on this porch with her tongue deep into my mouth? To tell the story completely to conclusion, get up without so much as a glance back, and then undress and undress the gardener Alexandra, who is just now weeding the lavender and jasmine?

Fassbinder, who came out to his father at fifteen, notoriously had suicidal lovers. One hanged himself in jail, another was found dead in Fassbinder's apartment. Ms. Schygulla herself, here in the role of Maria, was part of the volatile repertory company that included Fassbinder's mother. As for his homeland, he says, *Better a street-sweeper in Mexico than a filmmaker in Germany.*

And yet, ethically speaking, we don't miss Fassbinder's intentions. As Mirto says (do I break a confidence?), Jane, who is sane? What is sane? Mirto, an Italian woman whose name has a masculine suffix, a stone among stones — and thus true to herself — knows true power has few personal secrets, no ambition, and an occasional Russian princess. Although I too would prefer to be sweeping streets in Mexico, instead there are Spanish-speaking day laborers gardening below my Berkeley porch; the princess has gone home to her fourteen-year-old daughter.

The information that everyone wants, or wants to give, a blowjob, means nothing. Either we stop thinking of ourselves alone, or our fingers become ebony pincers, and there's no surprise when we open a vein of a testicle that is mistaken for a face we aren't allowed to kiss. One must individuate, yes, and then let one's self go, or one may miss two spotted fawns at the door at dusk. As two sharing the same right instinct, they are afraid of me. They are individuated, yet are one in this feeling.

A paradox that Mirto may have proposed. Again, I can't remember. I remember being afraid of you, of myself, of love, of my mother, of failure, of power, of powerlessness. Lashing out, and, in turn, taking your eyelashings. But after a year of ten years or ten seconds, I am afraid no more of you, my love, than the two fawns are of each other (not because I am special, but because I am a house in flames), all the while the fawns continue to fear me. They will never trust me. What has happened after observing a thousand blowjobs or tears, after studying the history of the ten thousand gas flames, after fucking the princess while the two spotted fawns spoke Russian with their large brown eyes, is that I remember everything poorly. As regards history, it's true, one cannot be trusted.

When you say you are no longer in love, I forget why. You would never let me shoot a fawn in the eye, and have it be found on my porch while I sweep streets in Mexico, and yet I am standing staring into their twin souls, and we trust my gaze on them as you never trusted it on you. That's a true story, and in the end, do you trust yourself to go where the opiate leads you?

The past doesn't help us. It goes missing. It confuses a testicle for a face. It confuses Fassbinder with Herzog, who filmed a great movie in a jungle, which nearly killed him. It is common that many layers of sediment will spill out of an important narrative, perhaps from an isle of the seafaring Ulysses, or perhaps one of Antigone's harmonious, dangerous acts will be lost. The surviving stories, with their tiny life rafts, carry us across history, across oceans of myth and meaning.

This is how I see it — over and over, separately or reunited, one of us glistens in bed, lazily, while the other thinks about having a smoke downstairs, after making love for hours,

long after midnight, somewhere in Berlin

x

I go crazy, wrong word, I get deranged, no, devastated, I have to take to my bed after seeing Lars von Trier's movies, which open nerves perversely, purposely. I hold my breath during the claustrophobic sinking of the train in *Zentropa*. Why must he have us blackout? Must we be party to his performance piece? Am I art? Is art life? Art and life, they have both tried to dislodge me. Night and fog, in Berkeley, feel like being underwater, on a night, in bed, metaphorically, with the poet Anne Carson.

Anne Carson is thinking about Paul Celan. I become aware, with chilling fever, of my American passport, my date of birth, my luck, and my grandmother's departure in a cargo hold. I slowly assimilate what Ms. Carson is absolutely, without doubt, aware of, that the phrase "Night and Fog" derives from a critical decision by Adolf Hitler and his staff not to conform to what they considered "unnecessary rules" for the deportation of Jews, Gypsies, homosexuals, the mentally challenged, and political agitators.

Where others have a mouth, lips, and a tongue floating from silken threads in the throat, to practice the fine arts of speaking, whispering, kissing, and singing,

on December 7th, 1941, SS Reichsführer Heinrich Himmler issues from the shit-hole of Hitler's face to order the following instructions to the Gestapo:

After lengthy consideration, it is the will of the Führer that the measures taken against those who are guilty of offenses against the Reich or against the occupation forces in occupied areas should be altered. The Führer is of the opinion that in such cases penal servitude or even a hard labor sentence for life will be regarded as a sign of weakness. An effective and lasting deterrent can be achieved only by the death penalty or by taking measures which will leave the family and the population uncertain as to the fate of the offender.

Adolf Hitler's malevolent wind *chi* issues a second memorandum, from a shithole that is now continental in size, through the barren Field Marshall Wilhelm Keitel:

Efficient and enduring intimidation can only be achieved either by capital punishment or by measures by which the relatives of the criminals do not know the fate of the criminal. The prisoners are, in future, to be transported to Germany secretly, and further treatment of the offenders will take place here; these measures will have a deterrent effect because - A. The prisoners will vanish without a trace. - B. No information may be given as to their whereabouts or their fate.

I cling to a bamboo reed of Anne Carson's poetry, *...the little raw soul / slips through. / It goes skimming the deep keel like a storm petrel...*

and learn from the scholar John Felstiner that Celan's parents refused to go into hiding and were taken to death camps. Celan's father supposedly died of typhus, and his mother by a gunshot into the back of her neck. I hold my mother's head up by the neck when she throws up, nearly expired. I cannot think, no, I cannot process, anything else. I am not a child who compares to the child Paul. I stop. He continues. A year after receiving the news of his parent's deaths,

he is in a camp himself. His German mother tongue, the *Muttersprache*, reminds him of the loss of his mother constantly. And yet, Celan is a poet who talks about being wounded by, and seeking, reality. From Felstiner, I learn more, that in January 1967, after a chance encounter with the widow of the poet Yvan Goll, Claire (who years earlier caused Celan's almost total breakdown by falsely accusing him of plagiarizing her husband's work), Celan tries to commit suicide by stabbing himself through the chest with a knife, missing his heart by an inch. Follows:

Celan writes "Temple-pincers" to describe the shock treatment he receives during nine months in a psychiatric clinic. Precedes:

his service as a psychiatric nurse.
Follows:

Celan, in his Bremen speech:

> Poetry is perhaps this: an *Atemwende*, a turning of our breath . . . is it perhaps this turn, this *Atemwende*, which can sort out the strange [*fremde*] from the strange?

He is aware that Adorno famously says that to write poetry after Auschwitz is barbaric. So he rejects one of his most well-known and difficult poems, "Todesfuge," "Death Fugue," which once had the word "tango" in the title, as still too descriptive of reality, of singing and dancing, speaking too directly about things that should not be said. For example, his "Night and Fog" describes the Auschwitz Orchestra, organized by the SS to play German dances and songs. No one of the singers survives the singing. Singing? He deranges his. Follows: "Die Ewigkeiten,"

> The Eternities went
> for his face and beyond
> it,
>
> slowly a blaze put out
> everything candled

We cannot assimilate this despair but we should study it, Anne Carson writes.

She quotes Celan,

> For a poet's despair is not just personal; he despairs of the word and that implicates all our hopes. Every time a poet writes a poem he is asking the question, Do words hold good? And the answer has to be *yes* [Carson's italics]: it is the contrafactual condition upon which a poet's life depends.

In Bremen, Celan says,

> It, the language, remained, not lost, yes, in spite of everything. But it had to pass through its own answerlessness, pass through frightful muting, pass through the thousand darknesses of deathbringing speech. It passed through and gave back no words for that which happened; yet it passed through this happening. Passed through and could come to light again, "enriched" by all this.

Within the word "enriched," "*angereichert*," (Celan's quotation marks) is buried the word "*Reich*."

Later in Bremen, later in re-civilization:

Keith Jarrett's gigantic, extemporaneous piano solo, during excruciating back pain. He goes from his hotel bed, to the concert, to the hotel bed. One of the single most beautiful, original works in the contemporary world, each hand playing the part of two hands. One lives, one aches, one vanishes; one cannot be compared to another. It is a sin. But does a violation of a moral code create a hierarchy of violations?

Northgate, dense fog, 9 p.m. – light's out, late

Miguel Palafox claims that he and four companions are approximately eight miles inside U.S. territory when, around 5:45 a.m. on May 12, 2000, two "rancheros" on horseback start firing at the group that wants to come to work.

According to the *I Ching or Book of Changes*, this is "Difficulty at the Beginning," the arousing thunder below and the abysmal water above. The name of hexagram #3, *Chun,* connotes a blade of grass against an obstacle as it pushes out of the earth. The hexagram indicates the way in which heaven and earth bring forth individual beings. It is their first meeting, which is beset with difficulties.

Miguel says that the "rancheros" are wearing Arizona-style ranchers' hats. He says that he is not able to determine whether they are wearing "uniforms." Miguel says that he distinctly hears three shots and that it must be the third one that hits him.

According to this hexagram,

> ...the situation points to teeming, chaotic profusion. When it is a man's fate to undertake such new beginnings, everything is still unformed, dark. Hence he must hold back, because any premature move might bring disaster. Likewise, it is very important not to remain alone; in order to overcome the chaos he needs helpers. This is not to say, however, that he himself should look on passively at what is happening.

It is believed that the U.S., as well as state governments, is now giving "license" to

Arizona vigilante ranchers to "hunt" for undocumented Mexican migrants on public land, which, in some cases is "leased" by the state to the vigilante ranchers. Migra Sector Chief David V. Aguilar, of *La Voz de Aztlan*, travels to the small border town of Sasabe on June 3, 2000 to interview the three sources to whom Miguel Palafox spoke.

Coincidentally, there are at least three implications behind the title, *Book of Changes*, according to Zheng Xuan, Eastern Han Dynasty:

> The fundamental law underlying everything in the universe is utterly plain and simple, no matter how abstruse or complex some things may appear to be.

> Everything in the universe is continually changing. By comprehending this, one may realize the importance of flexibility in life and may thus cultivate the proper attitude for dealing with a multiplicity of diverse situations.

> While everything in the universe seems to be changing, among the changing tides there is a persistent principle, a central rule, which does not vary with space and time.

Commander Pena, of the State of Sonora Police Department, states to *La Voz de Aztlan* that a young Mexican migrant worker named Miguel Palafox was hit by a high-powered explosive bullet that entered the upper part of his back and exited near his ear.

La Voz de Aztlan interviewed the owner of Rancho San Francisquito, Hector Nido. Señor Nido drove Miguel Palafox to La Clinica de Salud in Sasabe after Miguel showed up at the ranch with pretty much the entire left side of his face barely clinging to the cheekbone. Miguel arrived at Hector Nido's ranch at approximately 9:45 a.m. on May 12, 2000. Señor Nido stated that he was able to speak to Miguel Palafox during the trip to Sasabe, and that he could observe that most of the blood was in dry lumps, and it gave off a very offensive odor of decaying flesh. (Death itself stinks to high heaven.)

La Voz de Aztlan interviews Dr. Adel Aride Lopez, who treated Miguel Palafox and stabilized his medical condition in Sasabe, before Miguel was taken to the hospital in Caborca, Sonora, by State Police Commander Pena. Dr. Lopez stated that the bullet wound was serious and that there are indications that the bullet was "*una bala expansiva*," which are bullets designed to explode upon entering a human body. He describes Miguel Palafox's wound and corroborates both Commander Pena's and Hector Nido's statements. He states that the bullet blew off enough flesh that the thorax, cheekbone, and jugular vein were clearly visible,

as visible as dawn, as visible as a young, aging man scrambling from a large mesquite tree to a medium-sized ocotillo to a small bush of desert broom, which is named for its flowering head. It is extremely difficult to dislodge.

In the *I Ching*'s title, 易 (yì), when used as an adjective, means "easy" or "simple," while as a verb it implies "to change." In the hexagram, "Difficulty at the Beginning," the chaos clears up. A thunderstorm releases tension, and all things breathe freely again. Miguel crosses himself.

eight miles from Sasabe, 5:45 a.m.
I Ching reading, 1:11 p.m.

xii

The walk of friendship is littered. There's Robin's memory, I follow, of her mother, a nurse, looking terribly older in her graying uniform, and there's Robin's first husband, divorced long ago and living in a distant city, gliding by in the mental picture she draws for me of his white Mercedes. We *gringas* can barely make him out behind darkened windows and dark glasses. She recognizes the cock of his head; yes, she says definitively, *That's him, Jane, do you see him?* I see him for her, even though I'm crying and can't see anything. *Yes, there he is,* I say. That's his tan, lined face. We pass by actual, undocumented

workers digging holes and putting in yet one more drip system to monitor the timing for those of us of Tucson's foothills who need to water the indigenous cacti and illegal Meyer lemon trees and illegal California olives that we transport into Arizona, and, in the case of those of us trying to replicate lives from the other North American coast, grasses and roses. Here is Robin; she disapproves of anyone, with papers or without, working for her. Obediently, she's picked up an empty twelve-pack from the street. I admire her; it's as if she's walking her dead dog.

She tells her famous story, at the end of which are important syllables. The nouns and the verbs, the signatures of acts of betrayal and denial that parted the husband from the wife, and the wife from the husband, smolder in the dry air of the hill we climb. They trail off the trail, off the tail end of my own thoughts, *cheater, liar,* up, up, shortness of breath, little muscles gripping tight the vessels of the heart. The words of Robin's story several years old still burning. *Which is hotter, the heat of the day or the char of a love story?* I ask my friend;

I am remembering the day I asked. I turn and press her arm. She presses mine, says, *Keats, my man, I know you are suffering.* Have I earned the disreputable honor of crossing one of Robin's lines? She has promised to be honest, but now she is comparing my psychodrama to a great man's deadly tuberculosis. Or, she's joking. The fact that I don't know is not pleasant.

Camino del Sueño (Street of Dreams), 7 a.m.

xiii

Flossie and Rachel must move about Rachel's apartment very slowly because they are extended presences on earth. It is early summer in Westchester County, not far from where they spent much of their lives, separately, with men, with sons, with daughters. Elms have begun to bloom, late. There has been much rain, late. Sailing along the polished wood floors, Rachel is in slippers and Flossie is in tennis sneakers, her companions since her release. Rachel, the elder sister, matriarch of our family, has become irritable with a cold.

She is usually saintly, a diaphanous being who follows each neighbor's woe, with the gaze of her light blue eyes, to its signature end. She retrieves their stories for them when they ring her bell, the bell that rings for the night watch. She returns from night in the morning with dead papers, dead dreams, and sometimes, the dead themselves. Her nights are awful, busy, and reckless. Sometimes she listens to the radio. This night,

she sweats through her nightgown, and gets up, and falls by the side of the bed at 1 a.m., waking Flossie, my mother, next to her in the other single bed, scaring both of them, as they say now with conviction, *to death.* They sleep finally, and wake, and take a taxi together in a light rain to report the fever and the fall to the doctor. They do this. Rachel gets antibiotics to take her into her ninety-third year. As I write this, as it happens, that birthday is today.

After the fall of Rachel, and the doctor's visit, Flossie *repairs,* as she puts it, to the beauty parlor. She walks steadily, with a remarkable, albeit unconscious, confidence. Had this confidence, in all matters, risen to fresh air, how different the life would have been. Returning, she takes the shortcut through stiff grass, using a set of worn cement stairs, typical of those which front most of the old brick buildings of the sufficiently middle and lower middle class neighborhood. Flossie puts the key in the door with resolution because, having failed to remember it yesterday, she had been made to stand ringing for what seemed an hour, as Rachel slept. (*Can't hear well awake either*, her dead daughter, Barbara, remarks. Looks up from one of her canvases — she is working on a still life of red and green apples in oil — to admire her mother, as she was rarely able to do in time. She prefers to paint apples, arranging them carefully, and then, as was Cézanne's habit, at the last instant, turning them around. During Rachel's nap, Barbara takes another serious look at Rachel's closed blue eyes, as light and transparent as the sky after a little fog.)

The family favorite, Barbara left first, and occasionally paints the sky whenever the fog lifts and the drizzle ceases, and she has tired of apples and oranges, still struggling with differences in general, like life and death, or art and life.

Flossie has never heard of Cézanne, and is unable to comprehend why anyone would want to travel to Europe to see his, or anyone else's studio, after hearing what a dreadful time their mother Goldie had getting out of Russia on a cargo ship.

Can anyone's soul become more achieved by translating oils into Mont Saint-Michel, or into a bowl of figs, than by sliding onto a highly polished floor in sneakers with one's hair perfectly coifed, calling to someone loyally for 90 years, *I'm here. Where are you?*

Westchester County, afternoon

xiv

Where are we? Have we been airlifted into a remote area, a theater of operations where everyone is a suspect, everything is suspect? Or are we invited into a moment of grace, where it rains little copper bells? (Perhaps at one point we might have been responsible for them, and been changed by them.) Your grandmother hears them now, losing her mind, where it rains little copper bells. How they sound, resound, sound, frighten, and rain, before they are forgotten. (The name of the mother she has forgotten is Grace.) MaMa smiles, she stops smiling. The little copper bells are everything to her, and are gone. A gong, a teaspoon against a porcelain cup, a little melting sugar cube.

Alzheimer's, surreal time

39

xv

midnight, medication
6:30 a.m., medication
6:45 a.m., meditation and chanting
8 a.m., yoga
9:45 a.m., music
10:10 a.m., coffee
noon, cell phone, email
12:15 p.m., miso
12:30 p.m., Shiatsu
2:30 p.m., the beach

Eve does not want to leave the beach until the stars come out (her medication); no, Eve wishes to sleep on the beach overnight (her music); truthfully, Eve wishes to stay at the beach forever (her meditation). Eve is as dark as evening. (She is in many of the words I find on the beach.) Eve stops being young during the week she lives with me — this fact has nothing to do with me — while I am undergoing treatment in the Berkeley hills, in the heaven of Chinese medicine. Eve does an ode of her own yoga, repositions her protective eyewear, and recalibrates the raw materials of glass — sand, limestone, soda ash, and potash — first, at home in her mind, and then, in a molten oven heated above 2000°F.

The glass turns burnt orange and "fines out," allowing bubbles to rise out of the mass. She lowers the temperature because soda-lime glass stays plastic at as low as

1000°F. This is glass's zone of bliss. She works here.

Our yogi leads me, I must be led (plastic and workable), through a series of traditional poses, Sun Salutation A and Sun Salutation B, Downward Facing Dog, etc. I learn a little of the histories of India, China, Japan, and Korea, countries exhumed and subsumed, as the United States and as yet unnamed, denatured countries will again, in turn, resume and be consumed. As countries go, so go individuals, subsuming and resuming and powering and overpowering and educating and deceiving, in a long history of spurting blood by slicing one another's meridians with knives or bloody thoughts.

Eve won't walk on a beach unless she has somewhere to go, or if the beach is flat so as not to raise one of her hips higher than the other. The yogi is lying on her back, covering herself completely, and taking in the whole sun. She is so pale that I consider lying on top of her, breathing as she taught me, and without letting myself give off untoward sexual desire, as she taught me: we'd stood back to back, touching at our shoulders and hips. The surface of my body wished to touch her everywhere. My deep self did not, and prevailed. To shield her from a blazing sun, I might lie on top of her, facing the sun, and that might kill me, as it should, because it is possible I will move a muscle, and the sun god will burn out my eyes. Or god forbid, I will lie face to face, a thing I must do only, and as quickly as possible, by racing from the beach to my rented house and gift of a gardener, Princess Alya, a Russian endearment for Alexandra.

Eve goes to climb a giant rock, and the yogi and I fall asleep on a blanket on the sand. It is the sand and not the wool blanket that we feel, as we feel the center of the earth, gravity, and the pull of our innocence. I will only ever (there is the word eve hidden in ever, as it is hidden in love, and in here, and in sand) touch the bottom of the yogi's feet with my feet, which is very funny. I laugh for two minutes when it happens. Everybody does, all over the earth, on sand, or in bed, when they touch the bottom of feet to feet, lying on their backs, up on their elbows, knees barely bent, pushing with all our might against one another. Ha! I love you.

McClure's Beach, 3:30 p.m.
root vegetables, 8 p.m.
World Cup, 9 p.m.
medication, midnight

xvi

Penny and Rena are the patrons of the arts who miraculously have offered
me the use of the home they own next to their own home. They are the rea-
son I am acquainted with a gardener, a garden, a bed in the middle of my life,
and room for guests. Penny and Rena invite me and my guests, the glassblow-
er, Eve, and the yogi, Lisa, for Bandol rosé. Penny and Rena serve lamb
steaks, which we have never had, and the rosé, which I am not allowed with
the magic pharmaceuticals I am taking in order to be a person invited next
door, by Penny and Rena, for dinner, with the yogi and the glassblower.

The glassblower immediately looks for the hanging glass sculpture made to
order for Penny and Rena. I have seen the cascade of kinetic colors several
times, each time misidentifying it. The glass sculpture is paper! One seldom
knows what one is made of.

Next, the freshly showered yogi confuses a pair of Rena's slippers for an art
piece collected by Rena and Penny. The yogi looks a bit like the cascading
paper sculpture. I imagine that she has stood on her head many times. Her
hair is still a little wet, and she is so pretty I wish I could touch her, to steady
her, should she feel uncomfortable as an honored guest, being welcomed as
one who had, only recently, practiced her vocation of massage on Penny and
Rena. As for my steadying anyone, that is not right conduct, as the yogi does

her own steadying, and, as an acolyte, I am here to brush back the strands of my own hair.

Which doesn't exclude running my hands over a marble breast by Louise Bourgeois, a contemporary of Beverly Pepper's, and, as I did not know, the carver of the most expensive piece in Penny and Rena's collection. I understand, via Penny and *The New York Times*, that Bourgeois is recognized as the first sculptor "to turn the nurturing breast into a symbol of vengeance and aggression," whereupon I realize never ought I to have mixed the Bandol with the pills.

Eve said she would carry me next door if I cracked. Under no circumstances will I hold the sculptured breast to my breast, as I desire, in case it cracked (as I was drunk enough to crack it, but not yet drunk enough not to know which, at that late point in the evening, in life, would be preferable to crack, my mind, or the esteemed marble of Ms. Bourgeois).

Penny and Rena have kept a few of Kiki Smith's silkscreen-on-cloth dolls, *Lucy's Daughters*, while fifty are circulating the museums of the world. Penny and Rena show us their remaining ten daughters. No one knows how many Penny and Rena have, no one who counts (whereas the glassblower, the yogi, and I do not count), just as no one knows how many there are of anything, but we all know that number is reducing where it ought to be increasing, and increasing where it ought to be decreasing. Or perhaps I am only standing on my head. I hope so.

I certainly hope, as someone who is herself a daughter, that I can count myself fortunate, someday, that, rather than having circulated the world, I circulated a swimming pool with my mother. Even if the swimming was, as in Alice's case in *Alice's Adventures in Wonderland*, as Ms. Smith likes to remind audiences, in a pool of her own tears.

The exile, His Esteemed Dalai Lama, who knows this world better than anyone, and yet does not have the time to cry, did not authorize the seizing, sealing, delivering, and hanging of Tibet in a museum of a billion Chinese minds. *Such transactions are onerous*, the yogi said poetically and politically with her mind, and thankfully not to the collectors at the dinner table. They are not to blame for either a communist or a capitalist society that collects other countries. They wish poets were Percy Shelley's "unacknowledged legislators" in a world in which they, not incidentally, have been published by Rena on handmade paper, in one of her many art generosities. Rena, who is serving a handmade cherry tart and giving an exegesis on local, fresh produce.

As honored guests, and voluntary exiles, we ravish the tart, and then chocolate, gold-flecked, handcrafted truffles. Exposing myself as an ingrate raconteur, I give an exegesis on ownership and power while drinking from an empty glass, declaiming to those assembled, who needed no educating with a poeticism, that Tibet is in hell where it ought to be in heaven. The Chinese must take their own medicine, I pontificated, just as we all must.

Eve knows it is time to carry me next door. She would never drop me, although no one has paid any studio hours to mold and shave me, no one has collected me as Eve collects me in her arms. There is a very large plaster sculpture of a woman in the courtyard between Penny and Rena's front door and gate. She is one of their earliest pieces, and Penny has given her a name, which I can't recall, but I recall that Penny and Rena think the name hilariously funny, and I would do anything to have the honor of laughing with them, out of respect for their opulent generosity in all manner and matters, and therefore crack myself up.

She is bolted, as Penny explains, to the ground. I make a mental note not to allow this to happen to my mother, nor, come to think of it, to me, not even if we lose our minds and beg my brother, Fred, our power of attorney, to do so. The power of this attorney, Penny, has filled a tri-level space with shimmering colored paper, marble breasts, sheer photographs, floating installations, and reconfigurations of the female body, and Penny is laughing her head off.

In fact, I would like to spread Penny's generous guffaw all over the art world, the real world, the world of the dead, and the world of the mentally unstable, not one group of which can sharply distinguish itself from the others. There's plenty funny about these divisions, there may even be a Yiddish joke about it. The nut says to the artist, that's my garbage, or something to that effect. Much is lost in translation. Much is lost, period, that might have been saved, even transformed, by levity. While more and more people learn that we receive images through the eyeball upside down, only to have them reversed by the brain, only a few people know how to stand on their heads, gazing at emptiness, and that when all is in its rightful place, all is emptiness.

Northgate, midnight

The yogi, trained as a Shiatsu master, doesn't meet my gaze when she first wakes, appropriately. Preparation is all. Attention is required. I learn the point in the hand where the folded third finger presses against a crisis. I learn the ground is felt with the toes splayed and the four corners of each foot planted. She discovers on my head where foolishness knocked me at the shallow end of a pool. My master is swimming in the pool now. She has left me to my practice.

The Shiatsu master is a vase with pale blue irises when she works, legs folded under her, opposite me, as in a tea ceremony, which I am not quite prepared to attend, unfortunately.

Master, I am on our mat. Am following instructions. Unfortunately, am fortunately still taking prescriptions three times a day. Am not tired from the drugs, which means, unfortunately, I must stay on them. Poetry, fortunately, goes on and on, online, in chapbooks, hand-set, on handmade paper, and pressed into bark, while the proprietors of the small presses and their disciples assemble to open hearts from one end of the universe to the other, without need of me or anyone resembling me. Fortunately, this is a relief, even to those few who wept when I wept, and slept when I slept. Unfortunately, those who chose not to bow when I bowed have to find someone else to pour hot water on. Unfortunately, that will be easy, but fortunately, making such a gesture means they will never be masters.

Master, I am on our mat. I feel, as you proposed, my heart with my palms. I feel under my chin for the end of the heart meridian, and find many others there, who are, unfortunately, in much worse shape, and I'm ashamed of myself, and make tea for them, as you demonstrated every morning, which, unfortunately, I failed to observe keenly enough, and now imitate poorly, if at all, what it means to be a vessel.

The love that travels along the pathways of the body, may the sweet wind return it to you. May fortune have it that all your senses awake, through the breath through the nose, and may I apologize for filling the air with perfume too heady for one such as you. Fortunately, I love you too much to express it, having failed with a spray of the most exquisite Guerlain. If only I could spare you these outpourings, believe me, it is fortunate that I know that the tea must flow in one direction at one time to flow in all directions at once, I know but cannot say, cannot do. My energy, my master, disperses. Mellow white miso, koji spores, seaweed, daikon, ginger, beets, and other root vegetables, you wish them for me to ground me, as I wish you heaven on earth. If ever I were to touch you, fortunately it would not be on this earth.

Unhappily, if that is the right word, I have cracked the bowl of the one slave I am permitted to touch on this earth with a scream so high-pitched as to be inaudible, except that, unfortunately, she heard it, and lies in bed now with a new lover's hands over her ears. I pray that when her new lover moves down the pathways of my lover's body, that the unfolded third finger of love, my master, releases our crisis.

Ash Avenue, darkest part of the night

xviii

Because the world is over, because the world is lonely and we were going to be in
the same place, that's all... and that's why, although they never met, our dead rela-
tives introduced us. Now they have to live with what they've done,

gave us pleasure at the end of the world. They will see us naked, as at first, then
spent at the end of a beach. Theirs, and ours, is adult behavior as I understand it.
You seem neither as fragile, nor as violent as the waves, watching them, our relatives,
curl to shore like folds of brain. You seem drawn to science. What does the ocean say

about identity, as you consider the physical body that is offered you? Conditions
change, therefore, how can there be unconditional love, you ask. Naturally, you
make a brilliant point. You must think this is like fencing or heroin to stop

your heart. One day, we are hinged to land by a finger-tipped-sized spit. In a sec-
ond split, the world is over, in our case, metaphorically. That's all this is about: how
neither of us understood certain words or worlds of our elders. About love, about
making love, the world is over as we were

shown it. Our world's clover is slower.

North Beach, drunk, sunset

48

xix

Our sister is thrown from the back of a pick-up into a grave. Our grandmother loses her mind. We are Chinese, we are German, we are American.

Our brother is in prison. Our mother cries in a mental pavilion.

Virginia Woolf is homosexual and it drives her crazy enough to kill herself. This is what I think, but I am in an altered state (I have to be asked if I want to go into the treatment center Sierra Tucson); I enter a palace of pearls as my brother enters a banking institution. Both doors are made of water. We are water, we are death, we are in prison, we are mental patients, we are liquid jewels.

We house the liquid jewels in our pockets and walk into the river Ouse near Rodmell, in Sussex, perhaps because we cannot make love to anyone we want.

Virginia Woolf's mother dies when Virginia is thirteen. Stella, her half sister, dies two years later. Leslie, her father, suffers and dies a slow death from cancer. Her brother Thoby dies when she is twenty-four. She has her first prolonged mental breakdown. If, instead of winter, summer followed autumn, the journey of awakening would be a fantasy, as fantastic as Woolf's transforming of Orlando, from a man in the Elizabethan court, to a woman of 1928. The wilder the weather, the more ravens love it. If, instead of having an affair with Vita Sackville-West, devoted wife to the bisexual Harold Nicholson, Virginia could have had her for a lifetime, and had Leonard, her devoted husband, and Harold, Vita's devoted husband, taken others in marriage, would Virginia have lived longer? Happier? If, instead of rain and gloom, the English countryside were warm, would she have been too frightened to make love to a woman? If the English countryside were brighter, would she have been Vita's lover forever? The more conjecture in the wind, the more wind.

Let us never be too frightened to make love to anyone. After her final attack of mental illness, as scavengers have researched, and I repeat, please, not to sensationalize but, rather, to prevent anyone from nervous breakdown,

Virginia Woolf loads her pockets with stones and drowns herself in the River Ouse, near her Sussex home on March 28th, just before spring. *We could not have gone on discussing the nature of beauty in the abstract forever*, she writes in *Moments of Being*.

We are water. We are alone. We are a moment of being. We are introspective and anxious. We are mysterious and honest. We are groans, we are salty. We are winter, black water.

midnight

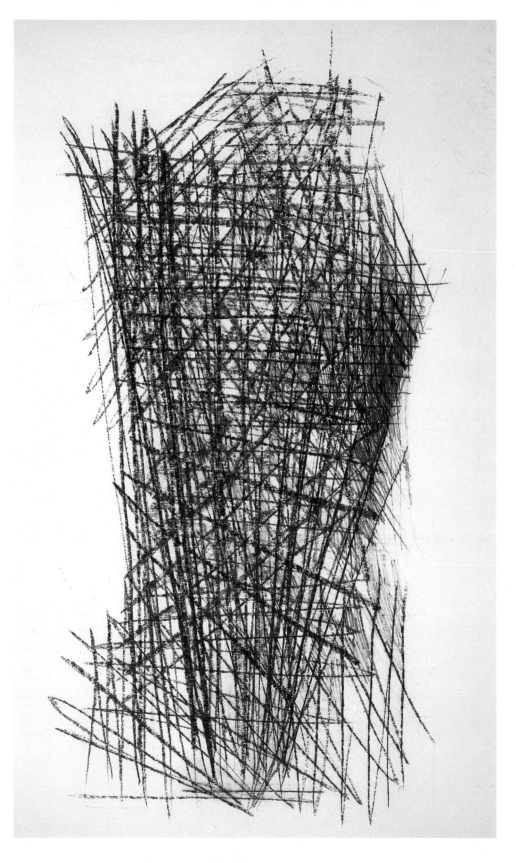

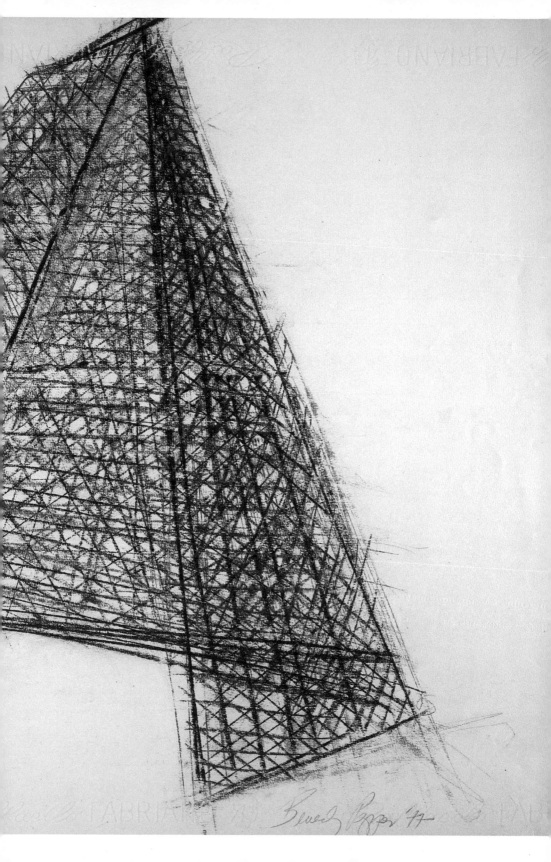

Second Night Under Water

It is not all right to be lying
          on a rose marble bathroom floor
                    of the divine Mandarin Oriental Hotel, ill,

without understanding why
                    your affections, after a long night of drinking and dining
          with friends, absent themselves from me,
                              about which I inform the toilet bowl,

and address your silk bed, because the door to it, and beyond, is ajar.
          Behold: your city view, your bay view, your dynasty, your snore.

I hate that you are unconscious
                    of your feelings for others, which allows you plausible deniability,
          once considered strictly a political foil, but presently

unpleasantly personal. Regrettably, my personal
                    vomit is staining the lotus
          embroidered over my heart
                              on the terry robe I shouldered in here in,
puking
          a meal we thought divine.
                              Courtesy of a royally
theatrical, full-blown panic
                    attack, it appears that, while we ate the same freshly murdered fish,
          only one of us can't stomach its prophecy,

that what goeth oneth under the table
                              may appeareth in all its nakedness anon.
          Therefore, please,

wake the hell up and get down here, on your youthful, aging knees,
                    and pray that we suffer
          our union together and survive it.
                              Repair

to these imperial marble tiles while it is still not terribly late,
                    while you still have me
where you want me, only subliminally
                              aware of your desire
          for whom you don't quite love or want.
                    Arise, you shit,

and recalibrate our timing with an unprecedented kiss
of my sick lips, and by your lights
sequester the future far, far, far away

in the fog of fucked-up relationships beyond San Francisco Bay.

Mandarin Oriental, Sansome Street, San Francisco, around midnight *xx*

Sailors disembark from battleships stalled too far from shore in shallow water.

The official record states that, "within ten minutes of the ramps being lowered, the company has become inert, leaderless, and almost incapable of action. Every officer and sergeant has been killed or wounded fording the water. There are about two thousand killed."

Your grandfather is a medic on one of the first boats to lower its ramp. PaPa sprints with a stretcher from one dead to another. PaPa takes eighty years to die. He sprints between narrow lanes of fire.

There are bushes, small trees. According to Chinese Taoism, we are wood, one of the five Chinese elements that is the basis of the universe. One learns from the *chi* master that there is access to a pure realm in which fear and hope are not known.

For example, the wood element is connected with anger, and a hostile person would be diagnosed as having an imbalance within that element. To alleviate the anger, appropriate meridians would be treated to restore balance.

My father leaps from a transport vehicle and breaks his arm. He eludes his scheduled departure on the ship.

We are sailors. We are Germans. We are embedded in steep terrain with our machine guns cemented into position. We have tremendous firepower with little range of motion. We are terrorists. We are wooden.

My father is ash, of stomach cancer. A painful way to die slowly, so he stops eating and drinking. Is he a suicide? Am I not here to assist him? Brien's father wasn't shot at, he shot himself. Are we not here to assist him? We have little range of motion. We are here. We are wood. We are writers. We are emotional. We decide. We shout. We are sour.

Samuel Beckett just turns thirty-nine when, in May, he's recruited to work in an Irish hospital in the French town of Saint-Lô, among the worst affected. The role of Clov, in *Endgame*, mirrors Beckett's at the hospital: keeper of painkillers. Desire, as the yogi teaches, does not lead to contentment. She returns to her mat.

If you are not a medic, returning to your stretcher, running back and forth with the dead, the better-off dead, and the ones dying for painkillers, and if you are not dead or dying for painkillers, you are commanded to sprint between narrow lanes of fire to scale the hundred-foot cliffs with ropes and ladders. You attack and destroy the guns at Pointe du Hoc.

Somebody smokes twenty cigarettes a day after surviving. Somebody's grand-daughter helps him pass. He dies of emphysema.

We are green. We are taking medication. We are liver, gallbladder, anger. We shop in the morning. We buy Camembert cheese. It is spring, Omaha Beach, Normandy. Jorie shows me the beaches and battlements near her home. We worry about her daughter. The next time we meet we are in Los Angeles, with her daughter. Her daughter holds me in her arms. I cry through lunch. Together, Jorie and I worry. She defends life staunchly, anxiously. We continue to worry wherever we are. World is an anxiety. Anxiety is a world.

spring, Los Angeles, 2:30 p.m.

I hear the singing of saws trimming overgrown trees. I am waiting at Northgate for the Russian princess to arrive to teach me about plants native to the region. Earth is nourishing, grounding, and family-oriented. This involves stability. This involves worrying.

I remember waiting anxiously for Kim. We were to meet after a separation. I arrive first (read: *low chi*). The spleen and stomach are involved, and I'm excited. Few remember Roger Williams, although we stay in the hotel in New York that bears his name. And since there was never a painting of him, many artists portray him by imagining him.

Some things are known. Williams cut a controversial figure (a strange double entendre) even as a kid in the parish of St. Sepulchre's, because of his horrified response to the burning of heretics at the stake, nearby in the British parish of Smithfield. Later, he preached freedom of religion. He sang, but people whispered. And so, in 1630, ten years after the Pilgrims landed at Plymouth, Williams thought it best to leave England.

Roger Williams eventually settled at the headwaters of what is now Narragansett Bay, and named his settlement Providence, in thanks to God. Thanks to God, whom I can accept as *chi*, our essence, nurturing our physical body, composed of the five basic forms of energy, one of which is earth, she arrives in a good mood. I'm taking notes about the hotel because I work as a journalist for her travel website. I am known to be hyperbolic and to make details up out of thin air. But I want to commemorate Roger Williams for the good he did on this earth, even though the hotel literature or, rather, its press release, prefers "The Roger." The release describes the outdoor terraces and rooms without addressing Mr. Williams, but rather Mr. Wassily Kandinsky, whose bold colors inspired the furnishings and quilts. Artists who make stuff up tend to get more credit than preachers who tell the truth. Because all we have is a mat in the middle of our lives,

because there is joy, there are laughs, and it is bitter, because late summer represents culmination or completion,

I am on my mat doing stretches on the floor of The Hotel Roger Williams, in New York, in March, and Kim has just showered. She smells of late summer, of lavender. I ignore her because we are constantly being transformed from one into another throughout the natural world.

The earth is caring, supportive, nourishing, and grounding. I rest on my back. I balance the earth on my pelvic bone. Kim takes me with a passion she has not shown in two years. I hear singing. She sings in the shower, when she cooks, when she walks from one end of the house to the other, between assignments, and in the car, especially after dinner out together, but this is the last time I hear her *after completion*, a phrase I acknowledge is the *I Ching's*, and not meant in the manner I affect.

Because all I have is a bed in the middle of a room in California, it is late summer. The gardener is late. It is late on earth. Sympathy is late, and singing is late. For a moment, there is stability. This involves worrying. It is late summer on earth. Princess Alya arrives. I am shown around an earth lacking Roger Williams. Lavender is everywhere. The yellow sun is complementary.

When I tell her this is the closest I've sat next to a stranger in a long time, she tells me to get on a bus. *You are not ready yet*, she says. She is nearer.

I meet the Shasta daisy, the Western sword fern, the coast live oak, barberries, buckeye trees, red salvia, Japanese maples, the California bay laurel (she says, *don't leave the laurel in the pot too long if you cook with it, because it is very strong*, but not to worry, I have no pot, no stove, no kitchen), and my old friend, the redwood. *Good to see you again. May I make lunch for you? Yes, on Thursday*. Sympathy is of the essence.

Northern California, two in the afternoon

xxii

A hot breeze caresses the leaves of the heavy maples. Tufts of Japanese mondo grasses wave slightly in the tiered garden. They look like black, lacquered seaweed.

As in Spain, or in Greece, or other southern Mediterranean countries, the summer heat now, in California, is worsened by the slightest stifling breeze. For some crazy reason, I recall F. Scott Fitzgerald's perfect description of wind through a summerhouse making things worse, the way he got curtains lazily billowing, and women perspiring in white, translucent dresses, and smoking. I'll never forget how perversely inviting the whole magnificent estate feels. As a reader, I remain outside, as I remain outside Hemingway. When Zelda cracks, or is cracked, or shock-treated into cracking — *bad wind chi,* as the Shiatsu master would diagnose — I invite myself in. A projection, Mirto might propose.

You and I have often been in southern climes, Kim, in heat exacerbated by wind, and have escaped into cool churches with other tourists to concentrate on Caravaggio's chiaroscuros. Outside again, the heat is crushing.

The heat of the day in these California hills slowly exits through recently opened windows. Large pink roses are braced to wooden slats. They face me as I face them. During the day, a pink that is nearly white, a white that is nearly milky. Now I am concentrating on them at night, and they are nothing to you, to whom I might have cried, *Look, look here! How alive!* The petals as soft as the faces of boys who stop by Caravaggio's studio, looking for him and looking for work; all the while, Caravaggio is painting a horse rearing up on its hind legs, about to crush a human form, as the lovesick intentionally crush a rose that has drooped onto a lane at the Berkeley Rose Garden. I take Eve there. She disturbs nothing. She uses her energy to shape glass into bliss.

The gigantic pink roses may as well be babies, finally crying themselves to sleep in the heat. My greatest shame is that I said that you should bury the idea of our ever having a baby. *Bury it*, I said. I had not yet buried anybody, nor did I understand the power of metaphor. Jews, do not go on burying a garment, not a thread, of someone you love because you think she has betrayed you.

Sir, unwell man, Mr. Mandelstam, excuse me for intruding on your afterlife, not who, but how many, betrayed you? In real, not psychological or metaphorical life, after you try to kill yourself, Stalin lets you choose to live in Voronezh. Here is your prophecy: "Only in Russia, poetry is respected — it gets people killed. Is there anywhere else where poetry is so common a motive for murder?" If it is through God, as it seems, that you write to us to change the world, then, dear God, what, my dear man, are you doing on a godforsaken train, and, then, good God, how do you manage to get a note to your wife from a labor camp near Vladivostok, near death, asking for warm clothes? Here, please, let me cover you. Let us all cover you with our bodies. Here are your warm clothes.

Silently, we are still here. By we, I no longer assume you. By we, you now mean whom?

Of dreams, we are not dreams, my love. We are large pink roses on the side of the house. Action, not memory, we are braced to wooden slats. We live in the world, in the heat. We are silence, we offer our indescribable perfume, scenting a large bed in the center of an otherwise empty room. We are nothing else on earth. We are over-sized pink roses, so light a pink that we are nearly white, invisible. (I am braced to you.)

North Berkeley hills, middle of the night, life / afterlife

A German and a Jew give birth to a dead baby. There is grief and sadness. The image is white, ashen. We are Jews in Amsterdam in 1936. We are Germans in Amsterdam in 1936. We are precise, meticulous, with a tendency to pessimism. There is weeping. Contraction, accumulation, self-control. It is evening.

Kim and I go to the Anne Frank Huis. It is a new millennium. There is still hope. I weep uncontrollably. Kim weeps.

As the world remembers, Anne and her family live in an annex of the building at Prinsengracht 263 for more than two years, where Anne's father, Otto Frank, has his business. The Van Pels family and Fritz Pfeffer also are hiding there.

A moveable bookcase conceals the doorway to the annex. The office personnel know of the hiding place and help the eight people by supplying them with food and news. On August 4th, 1944, the hiding place is betrayed, and slowly, over the course of a century, the story goes around the world that the people in hiding are deported to concentration camps. Only Otto Frank survives.

We read Anne's letters; they are prose poems of daily existence. Upsets, jokes, meals. God knows how she writes, God knows she needs to. God? Is that now just an expression, like, who in hell knows why? Or, who knows wherefore thou fucking are, God?

On a local level, Kim is very upset with me because I have "shot my mouth off," a crude expression from my childhood streets in New York, not lost on a writer who knows the danger of sensationalizing language. I have slammed her family as I would slam a ball with a stick out of my childhood. I would get down into the gutter of language in search of the lost ball of that childhood, which has rolled deftly and inexorably, like childhood itself, away and down. Stickball halts until I lie my face on the sewer grating and pluck out the hard pink Spaldeen with a deconstructed hanger. *Bigots*, I called them, which they were not,

they were kind; they held me in their embrace until I became one of their family, more than my own family embraced me after the idyll of childhood took a hit with a wrecking ball of adult behavior. Bigots, completely uncalled for, a grave and sacrilegious error, a *transference.* She is so upset in a restaurant that she cries and cries and we must leave. She is so upset in Amsterdam's Okura Hotel, in De Pijp, that she wishes to crack the glass of the skyscraper, where our bedroom is on the seventeenth floor, and leap to her death.

I happen to read an item, as I am writing this today, online in the *Amsterdam News*, that a woman was murdered last week on that same seventeenth floor of the Okura. This chills me, and brings home that I could have lost Kim, because I know that she is thinking suicidally, while I go for a swim in the heated pool at street level. God help me — another way of saying: who in hell do I think I am? — from the glass swimming pavilion, I might have seen her drop to the pavement. This is a private, true story. I am ashamed to write it. Why must I? Do I think I am a Jew in Amsterdam in 1944? — who betrayed them? who panicked? Who? I am so sorry.

We will never be Jews in Amsterdam in 1944, *thank God*, as my mother would say. *Lord have mercy*, as Kim would say. Are God and the Lord two different entities? Who in hell cares, with millions of lives uncared for. Kim believes neither in the Lord, nor in God, which perhaps can be dated from when her young lover was murdered. Kim was fifteen. This is a private, true story. Why must I write it? Another transgression on a local level. Why? I am searching for my lover in public places, in low light.

She has not forgiven me. And worse, I seem to be comparing my pain to the pain of Anne Frank, times millions of Jews, and I should be reprimanded for the transgression. Being locked in a metal car has been my recurrent nightmare. Also, that I am taken to a shower to my death. I have, as Mirto proposes, identification issues. Marginalization issues. Outsider issues, police state issues. Ordinances issued in the "name of the people" issues, and so on. Relationship issues. One thing issues forth —

Kim permits herself to go on with our journey a while longer. We do not know the Dutch. We admire their lace curtains, a transparency that invites us to gaze into the refinement of their living spaces, especially those at street level, as we walk the city. We do not know people.

The floating flower market is nearby, on the Singel. It is a white evening, it feels like autumn, but it is spring. It is raining hard. I betray her without taking another lover. I leap from her heart into a brown canal. Why should she fish me out? It is not high drama. I can shower in our high-rise hotel. She does not leap suddenly from the seventeenth floor. Rather, slowly, she betrays me, a network of canals we get lost in. I lose her in Amsterdam, in Normandy, I lose her in New York.

Do I think her suffering, or mine, requires public scrutiny? We are responsible for our own suffering, therefore we are pathetic, not tragic. We know the difference, believe me. But why trust me? Because I am, like you, deeply disturbed,

for reasons obvious to anyone still remotely interested in the life of this city, about what went on under the low clouds of this lowland? There is yet one more murderer to apprehend, who simply took the elevator with his weapon concealed. It is written of on a local level. This is history,

which includes the hiding and betraying of neighbors. And this is history: When we see the finished, cut, polished jewels on Paulus Potterstraat, we buy ruby and diamond earrings. Compensatorily — although we know such is not possible — we attend our own nightmare in a cave (as we might attend an art film at Pathé Tuschinski near the Rembrandtplein) heavily compromised by insufficient oxygen, in virtual darkness, save for lamps belted to Black African foreheads. What is hidden? Who is hidden? Where is the historian who will unearth the miners?

Some tragedies may be uncovered; the murderer on the seventeenth floor might be punished, live in a cell with metal bars. Perhaps he will be killed. He will be disappeared. Who will unearth the conscience of the law? Metal is one of the five Chinese elements that is the basis of the universe. The lungs and large intestine are involved, in terms of Chinese medicine. It is difficult to breathe. There is not enough oxygen on earth. The endangered are breathless, running, or holding their breath, hiding.

I want to go home and forget, but one must not forget. Kim wants to go to the torture museum to view iron maidens, guillotines, and hanging metal cages. Neither gets what she wants.

Amsterdam, 5 p.m., already very dark

xxiv

Mirto says you have been afraid of me because you are afraid that I will die, and so you have accommodated your unconscious by leaving me for someone else. You always have had to have something, or someone, else, on the horizon, like a plane seen from a great distance, which you keep an eye on and thus do not have to meet my gaze. Yes, what a terrible demand that must seem, with your eyes on the sky. I understand this turning a blind eye to me.

Permit me to express, I am so, so sorry that someone horrible, someone evil and godless, murdered your first love. I would like to personally kill him, with a powerful weapon, but all that I possess is imagination; I would go back there if I could and re-configure destiny.

I would like to take his high-powered rifle and fire it — shall I hold my tongue? I swear to Jesus godforsaken Christ, from the same overpass, in the fog, when he's driving to his parents' house, Christmas Eve, and kill him through the back of his Pinto's trunk through the back seat through the front seat through his heart. Here: everyone involved thought it at one time: *kill him*. Now I have said it, biting my tongue at the same time because I am breaching a confidence; I am telling your story, and hers, which, by your moral code, is strictly forbidden. God forgive me. God, who killed Rhonda?

He needs to be dead. Even if he's just some sickness, out firing at nothing, once. He has killed someone, and he has killed something in you, and I want him dead.

I know you are against the death penalty. I would hope to be. But first I must kill someone and then perhaps someone will kill me. It's none of my business, but self-ishly, now that I am heartless, I want him to be, too.

I lie in wait. If I am shadowing him, am I not he?

What do you imagine happening? Does anything happen imaginatively, or are we predictable? You don't love me anymore. Yes, it's unconscious isn't it, but I am the murderer. Psychologically, I have killed something. But the fact that I also want to kill him means I am ill, am I not?

Valdese, North Carolina, 2 a.m. – 3 a.m.

xxv

It happens that I fly toward a new job in a distant city every Wednesday, I fly away from it every Friday. Flying alongside me is what my shadow does well. The rest of the time, the shadow tries and tries and cannot die. In flight, a shadow also represents the larger body of the plane, and covers the bed of land with a black, starched sheet. In flight, the shadow follows the plane as night follows day.

Sadly, the shadow cannot reach over for a kiss. Happily, I was able to kiss you when you got over your fear of flying and acknowledged my existence. Holding hands, whispering, kissing — three sisters whom I see reflected in the dark window.

You rush, below. You have silence's mindless, bare feet, and rupture's scar at your lip, and mistrust's habit of smelling food and wine before eating and drinking. You are on your way to sleep, eat, make love, dream. When you go to work, driving yourself, rushing, with papers flying, the plane seems not to move.

Its descent brings out a whole village of dreamers and lovers and liars and cheaters, and the silent and broken ones, in a circle on the ground below. They seem, but this is only conjecture, from their waving and praying, bent in shame, helpless, to be waiting for an answer. Over and over, we are brought down by everyday events, utterly disappointing everyone. We arrive at the same place, same time, o my brethren.

This has not been a flight of fancy. I want out. Fly by, night.

Sometimes the plane appears to fly backwards, to an earlier time. The passengers change their watches. I don't want to go there, but I go. I go forth. Going back and forth, back and forth, as I have for many months, making shadows of light, darkness of white clouds, is very moving, symbolically, of course, but not always literally. For example, upon my return home, happiness — at seeing the neon orange letters T-U-C-S-O-N spilling vertically down the flight tower — momentarily floods my senses, but the plane lands safely. Moonlight floods the runway, but we need not drown.

Houston-Tucson, *Continental Express* flight #2047, arrival 8:30 p.m.

xxvi

You and I, completely separately, sense real happiness is beyond us. Happiness is a freak of nature, an eel slithering toward the Texas marshes where I have landed again, a fly-by-night friend, here, and then gone into the greasy Katy Prairie, which yields half a million muskrat pelts, worth four hundred million dollars annually to the fur industry. If you thought about it at all, this is perhaps not what you thought I learned working in Texas. Of all the things I could say, given an opportunity, I scare you with furless muskrats. I never know what to say, at a time like this, with an eel in the sealed chamber of my mouth;

now that I have opened a conversation with you, it continues on course, with the plane on the ground in Houston, toward the watery edges of civilized life. I ask out of bankrupt emotions, matter-of-factly, whether we're going to make it. One of us, I see, has made it, but I see her from so far that I fear I'll never find the end of this dark, marshy water. It is midnight when I begin to cry, a young pink cry. Is that you? No, it's Paul Celan:

Speak —
But split the No not from Yes.
Give your say also the sense:
Give it the shadow.

Give it shadow enough,
Give it as much
As you know is assigned to you between
Midnight and midday and midnight.

Why must I swim alone? Each piece of the night sky shatters around me. My lungs fill and empty; I swallow a few stars. By the time they ought to sustain me, they are minute, terribly old. Where stars are bright until they fail, the heart is hidden, darker than a thought. If my eyes are closed, there are flares in the night. If I open them underwater, I swim to the end, and I miss my mother.

Keith Jarrett's *La Scala* on iPod; reading Anne Carson's translation of "Spruch Auch Du," *Continental* flight #67, Tucson-Houston, arrival 3:30 p.m.

xxvii

It's my birthday, and the last night Kim is celebrating with me at table, accompanied by two friends, and my former best friend, with whom I have, yesterday, reconciled, and therefore I deliberately make a toast to the effect that this is the strangest party I've ever had.

A toast from a blue bottle of costly European water and an anti-anxiety pill so as to appear to be someone standing, walking, and living. It has only been since I've been an adult that I have been given parties for any reason. My mother on one occasion recognized my birthday with a celebration, and it was duly photographed, with cousins and neighbors and, in the background, the little globe of floating objects my brother's friend cracks. He lofts it and looks away. The way one might look away and miss being kissed, or miss purple clematis among bright green, freshly rained-upon vines.

In the party photo, there is Jill, my first crush, and Diane, whom I boss around, and, too, the infantilized twin boys from across the courtyard who I watch get undressed by their mother when she neglects to draw the shades. I wait for these nights; these are the moments of mystery across a real courtyard, rather than the stifling, transsubstantial antechamber between my brother's bed and mine. Because the twins still sleep in beds with protective sides, and their mother raises the bars to undress them, it is very difficult to see their penises.

In the black-and-white photo, the broad dresser where my brother and I store our underpants, socks and t-shirts, stands guard over the group in their little dresses and pressed pants. Maybe I am seven. Many mornings I watch my brother get dressed, without really seeing him. His is more like a torso in a dream.

In any case, it is under the melodramatic circumstance of having moved out, like a torso disappearing inexplicably and naturally from a dream, that my ex purchases tickets for a concert after my birthday party. This is to initiate a period which, in her mind, would mean that, though separated, there will be no rupture. An idea, among many, that is unrealistic and delusional, if pleasant.

Therefore, we hold hands during Cat Power's nervous hand-wringing and beautiful, warbled singing for some two hours. Tall and thin, and meagerly dressed, the singer moves like a daddy longlegs around the stage, and then more like her namesake, pouncing her slender body a foot or two this way and that, disorderly, nearly maddening. She never flirts with the audience and keeps her legs carefully closed under her mini skirt as she swivels on the piano bench, at one point to receive applause after playing a stunning solo, accompanied by her same haunted, perfectly pitched, soft, near cry. This song, and a last, *a capella*, softer one, quieted the hall such that the audience breathing became her orchestra. We musicians possessed power I will never forget, although I cannot remember the names of the last songs, nor their words. At one point, I remember thinking, *Who is singing? What is singing? Singing is writing amplified*, I thought; I'm on meds. Kim is drinking, I hope she's drinking piss water;

whenever she drinks from a plastic cup, she is in a dubious situation. She has lied about something, or someone, and justifies it on the basis of my temper when I recognize the lie. As my brother thinking the distance is enormous and no one can see him undress.

Cat Power, Rialto Theater, Tucson, 11:30 p.m.

xxviii

Lisa once told me she was a jaguar, black spots inside black circles on a tawny coat. Did people know —

I ask myself while practicing lying on my back and throwing my legs over my head, arms raised and my index finger last, as Lisa taught me to go down the rabbit hole, pointing toward the heavens —

that you are the reason, my darling pig, and not my sorry cotton-tailed ass self, that our gay husbands divorced us? All along, I thought I must be the reason, lonely, resting, not cooking, just drinking and puking, going to bed early, asking the guests to leave, nearly letting my favorite, *o but what was her name?* of their dogs drown, playing the piano without distinction, sobbing over nothing, screaming My Father Is Dead, so Brien could scream My Father Shot Himself In His Kitchen And I Had To Fly To My Parish To Clean The Blood Of His Brains Off The Wall, all the while thinking, they hate me, I am a fake poet, I am a fake Jew, I am a fake lesbian, I am a fake teacher, I am a poor swimmer and a worse cook, I cannot drink for shit without puking, I came to Champagne late in life, I drove too slowly on our vacations together through Italy, I swam naked with them even though I was fifty, how terrible that must be for gay men, and also, and perhaps most evidently, I did not try to find out why; I let you write the postcards and call them and beg.

Our husbands, a lion and a lamb, dine and drink and swim with us with a family of Chihuahuas — Laverne and, *o my god, what was my favorite's name?* This is how terrible life is, for the moment, for eternity, to forget one's beloved's name, whom I held in my arms. While you and our husbands cook and drink in our kitchen, night after night, hold her in my arms until she trusts me, which is all love is. We play games, although the gentle lamb always wins.

Each picks a card with a name on it and holds it to his or her forehead so everyone else can see who's there. We play rounds and rounds. We pour rounds and rounds. I lose. You lose. Brien loses.

When our husbands call me at the Houston Hilton after their late dinner on Kauai, the friendly lion roars his revelation over the phone and the ocean. They saw you kissing a girl in your car, and not kissing me in our house, the chilled cocktail that freezes my brain and heart. Now they are calling me on it, and about it. And I am an asshole, like the circle at the end of the barrel of a gun

with which Brien's father blew his brains out onto the kitchen wall in a house in a parish that flooded so that none of this any longer exists:

Brien's dead mother stood trial for serving liquor to minors already on prescription drugs, one of whom nearly died, and you accompanied him to St. Bernard Parish, as his wife (in everything but name and act), and the courtroom was hot and humid, and the trial lasted all day, and she was acquitted because she said, to no one in particular, that her husband blew his brains out, and then you drank straight whiskey out of paper cups. I've always been meaning to ask — even though this is exactly the sort of question, unaccompanied by segue, that you detest enough to leave me — during some humid, endless day, do you ever think about being someone else rather than being *with* someone else?

via Kauai, around midnight / St. Bernard Parish, Louisiana, 9 a.m. – 5 p.m.

xxix

Between hope and despair, a large house in the desert sits empty. The wind, from time to time, thrums the grand piano, even though the piano is shut tight. And the windows are sealed, so the alarm rings and rings, and no one responds.

Mice are no longer saved who have fallen into our saltwater pool in the hours before dawn. They descend to the bottom. Mostly babies. The manager of the dead comes once a week, Tuesday mornings at 7:30, and lifts them out with a net and puts them in a dark pouch. Where do they go from there?

Once, on the wrong anti-depressant, you became hysterical about bugs in the pool, each one of which you needed to save. I thought I was strong, and could help you, could see that your sympathetic nervous system was flaring, because you would at any cost, the cost of your own life by drowning, need to save them, the flies, the mice, the snakes, the butterflies, the swarming bees. And many were saved but not all. And finally you saw this was inevitable, this was living and dying. I never could help you, although I lived through all your hysterical ailments. Your brown eyes did not want me to help. Eventually I turned away, and now my gaze goes from the inside of my head to the night sky and skips your gaze entirely, as you willed it.

If a person would lie to the person she loved because she had to, because circumstances were such, then it is in character that this kind, hospitable liar would trowl down to the bottom after a helpless Chihuahua, a prehistoric looking creature who has made an egregious mistake that could cost her life only because she was so thirsty. In your right mind, every thing and everyone was worth saving,

but the more we tried, the more saving and loving each other became incompatible. In the end, it is a fact that you lifted a young and therefore highly venomous snake to safety, and inflated the flat, depleted moon, when it fell into our pool, and returned it to the heavens, calmly, responsibly. In a culture that is unaware of poetry's magic and its mythologies, I beseech you — you who once wrote poems, which is how you no doubt came to be a familiar of celestial bodies — please, become one of the helpless who did not mean it when she said, *you sad peripatetic moon, I am no longer in love with you.*

Separated from you, I see the frown of crescent moon, so you have not taken up the request. When it lowers, slowly rocking, and finally falls, I can return you the favor, sincerely, and put it back where it belongs, as I suspect you always hoped I would, and despaired that I was not capable. Granted, it is merely a shaving. The rest is in darkness.

Thank goodness no one can see me looting the dark pouch for the dead mice.

Northgate, midnight

76

Last Night Under Water

The last of our sunshine returned
        today from your abandoned place;
                our friend brought our black lamp and other stuff over.

It seems like you're dead; I could be in love
        with someone else. *What has happened,*
                as Rufus Wainwright's lyric asks, *to love?* I am nothing

if not melodramatic, and God knows that
        I listened to that song you burned me, a hundred round trips,
                earning a living forgetting
you. You
        know I exaggerate, but I do remember

buying inconsequential, beautiful cups,
        a yellow couch, a purple chair, a bed of foam, etc.
                Separately, they took up residence,

like I settle into a crouch, self-centered, oblivious
        of my maker, and think,
                Go to sleep, Jane, or make yourself sick. Or

call your new passion, and recall the abandoned place
        where you promised a black lamp
                it would become a sentimental cup

of tiger light.
        Lift her brown hair until she slowly undresses
                a hundred flames,

                        and finally lets you wet her
unbelievably floral
        countryside,
                burning native olive
                and oak.

And there's a finely tuned piano, and purple wine.

Christmas Eve / morning, Napa Valley, 1 a.m.

It's a small beach. The water's cool. Cold. Better to set a small craft sailing than swim. When across the bay, we look back to its sandy shore from Tony's, where they grill oysters. If the fog's not in, we're absorbed, from the beach or from Tony's, by the bobbing oyster beds, which are protected by wire cages. Perhaps you are thinking of the oysters as having a briny nose, as wine is said to have an essence, or are considering their fresh and saltwater incubation, because you identify the ingredients of food and drink before you swallow. Who knows? I fantasize their pearls.

We don't sail or swim from the beach; we learn there are sharks. It's just a strip, really. Aesthetically, but also philosophically, this pleases us, confirms our insignificance in the universe; and nobody's ever there, at least this time of year.

A few Octobers later, I return, to a grocery store just past Tony's, which has a couple of bleached benches out back overhanging Tomales Bay, even closer to the water than Tony's, and have a huge plate of oysters and a beer, and sit here. Warm autumn afternoon. Soon a slow, cold fog will come in, and tomorrow is supposed to be warm again, climate that produces a delicate dessert wine from late harvest grapes. You told me, I forget, are the best Hungarian?

I'm working at a writer's retreat up the road, at the Marconi Center — remember, I used to think it was Moscone, named for the San Francisco politician who, along with Harvey Milk, was murdered.

No, it is Marconi. He was expert in radio signals and waves. Marconi is credited with locating survivors of the Titanic disaster, who were forcibly broken out of their embellished oyster cage, I can't help thinking, clustering my thoughts together. I lean on the splintered rail overlooking the slender bay toward the beach and its shallows. The day's warmth gets inside my sweater. Then, I walk back very slowly, full of the details of earth's rotting work, and man's constructions — which affirms that a world can exist beneficently — a day before you puncture me, like a grape, with one of your lies.

I have arranged to meet you at a hotel in the city after my job, but something gets me out of the car at the last second. You tell me, when I call to cancel, you are terribly disappointed, but, soon thereafter, that, actually, you have flown out earlier in the day, and are already in a far city, nowhere near the San Francisco where we were to have slept together. The room I sleep in all week, and that last night, has a high ceiling whose blistered skylight distorts light. Dusk, dark, dawn, distorted.

It is again a cold day, in the imagination. Everything looks different. As if clusters of tiny, pale gold, sick, cold grapes have been added to a black-and-white photo of a winter vineyard.

They look like pebbles, or petals, from this distance, this year. What beautiful words emerge from memories — pebbles, pearls, oysters, grapes, and petals. Why bother with metaphor? Is not each word, in its own furious existence, like a perfume, different on everyone?

Which reminds me of the Fracas you wore so operatically, with tuberose, gardenia, jonquil, and hyacinth in its top notes, jasmine, orange flower, white iris, and peach in the middle — the perfume is known for its long middle breath — and sandalwood, cedar, musk, and vetiver for bass notes. It could be drunk out of a stemmed, clear glass. It makes me drunk. If you ever read this, perhaps while thinking, or drinking, or half drowsily thinking and drinking, a faint, dolorous sensation — of music, of language? — will cut into you for a moment, and you'll get it — what's left of what I feel — shark.

Heart's Desire Beach, Inverness, lunch break

xxxi

How far is it from a midnight of palaces leaning, fish staring, gulping the air of the shallow waters of thought, of feeling, where we look out toward the watery castles and floating glass mirages and see the whole moat lit by shimmering headlamps

the past, Venice, 11:55 p.m.

to something that may be issued in a dream, the only place in which I trust to meet? If only I could get there.

How many times you walked from our bed completely asleep, muttering, confabulating, crashing into walls. How we barred the windows and doors on high floors, shoving an armoire when our room hung over a steep cliff, in preparation for your nightly journeys. Are you there yet? I hope not. By God, I hope not. Twice, you damaged a shoulder and tore your knees trying to get there. A couple of mixed drinks, a late night out with friends, and you crashed into a door and wall of our bedroom, dark with moonlight.

What a strange dream I was in the whole time — dropping into a church, when night arrived, like the head of a horse with leather blinders — listening to you walk and talk in your sleep, and believing every word. Your sleep often seemed disturbed, disturbing. Much later, the culprit, love, was captured, allowing us to see the thing entire, the pitted gums and sausage-like intestines. "It," by now, is a monstrous thing, out of place, in the water, on the street, in bed, in battle, in hell, in a nightmare. In a hotel,

I'm daydreaming a while. It hurts no one, nothing, only this white sheet. And now, this white sheet of paper.

Hell (according to Sartre, "any Wednesday, 3 in the afternoon"), daydream, Hilton Hotel, Houston, 3:33 p.m.

Kate tells me The Rothko Chapel receives meditators all the time, some of whom bring square, sequined pillows and kneel stationed, as though before a Station of the Cross, before his giant, violet blue masterpieces. A couple is bent before Rothko's northwest panel when we arrive. We are dressed for dinner and pillowless, mentally and physically not prepared to kneel. Kate is better, having not been well. These euphemisms: *better, not well,* are common among mental patients, which I consider both of us to be, though neither is at the moment. She is no doubt thinking, and rightfully so, if she is thinking of this at all, that I have a hell of a nerve discussing her case, discussing her as a case.

As an artist, she is deeply moved by the process, the grandeur, and the feeling of the Rothko violet panels, which fill the space as contemplation fills the mind, emptying the space, filling the space, emptying. Kate's face has the glow of a Chinese fire-eater I remember embroidered on the back of a jacket of someone I loved long ago. I go back there as I go to the violet blue paint; each serves as a medium for making life into art and art into memory. In memory, she lightly scratches my back for what seems hours. I live for the instant life loses its bearings in a private passion or a public, physical work of art.

Kate and I move about the chapel trying not to disturb meditators lost beyond thought. Kate and I are restless, lost in thought. I know I shouldn't speak for her. I have discovered little about Kate, despite knowing that she makes miniature, handmade books at twenty-hour stretches, often without eating or sleeping, and does not mind being alone. She says she gets depressed, but that being around people often brings on the depression. I told her I am sick of, or from, being alone; I can't remember which. She shrugged.

Inside the Rothko Chapel, a violet middle panel weeps; on each side, night falls on a darker, midnight blue panel of the watery beginning of time.

Rothko claimed not to have been an expressionist but "was interested only in expressing basic human emotions... The people who weep before my pictures are having the same religious experience I had when painting them." Kate is not sure of me, I feel this. Yet she lets me lie on her mat when I visit her.

The Chapel commission writes, "Rothko's output reveals darkness as a fundamental note in his repertoire, a reminder that an involvement in light presupposes an acquaintance with shadow..." The young couple on their knees looks "blissful," a feeling engendered how, Mr. Rothko, weeping your way through the making of these gigantic rectangles and knowing others weep with you?

Better to see the chapel in natural light, we were told. Yet, here it was dusk, and we were very happy. In my case, tears of Happiness: that euphemism for not being unhappy. Or, Happiness: a spirited experience of great release, a cry, an emission, an admission, of what kind? Admission into what? Bliss, Mr. Rothko, a kiss in the dark? A sense of the broken whole? A fuck you addressed to death? The feeling of something beginning with no end? Making a painting, a triptych, a whole octagonal room of floating, violet, giant pages, a handmade book, a life, without stopping?

Montrose, dusk

85

xxxiii

The Gobi, Asia's largest desert, or dry sea, is famous as the site of several cities along the great Silk Road, a long, saffron moebius strip in the Western imagination. It is an old road, from Sappho to Marco Polo to Bashō, and beyond. Camels give birth in Gobi, in Inner Mongolia, China, every March. Two filmmakers, traveling through, find a family who own twenty pregnant camels here.

But when Falorni and Davaa return to Mongolia in March to produce a documentary, they meet a wild snowstorm in Ulaan Baatar. When they finally arrive at the nomads' *ger,* most of the camels have given birth. Four generations live in the same *ger,* a bright orange nomad's tent. It's the color worn by the esteemed Dalai Lama, and also used by Christo when he designed nylon gates for Central Park.

Art and life do not collaborate until the very last birth. Typically brown, the last colt is white. And when the colt's mother rejects it, the filmmakers have their story. Those who feel that a documentary, or in this case, a documentary with some scenes recreated, brings us where we have no business, and furthermore, those who feel that a documentary that condenses time (because it is art), is somehow suspect, may be right. I cannot quarrel with them. And yet, to lose oneself in its time is to see a fire red blossom, as real as an insight, suddenly appear in a desert one thought one knew well.

Brightest of all, paradox, too, may be suspect, serving both art and life, but let us not quarrel with mothers and grandmothers who love their children yet sometimes are horrible to them, ignoring them for who knows what reason. Perhaps later in life, as the story goes, the boy who hid behind his mother's skirt will become a great Spanish matador.

The camel keeps walking away from her colt, the colt won't stop crying, even if someone tries to feed it a bottle, the camel will eventually die without its mother's milk, and so we have a story requiring attention, *The Story of the Weeping Camel.* One mystery to be revealed is, to which camel does the weeping refer?

A musician is summoned who plays the *morin khuur,* a two-stringed instrument. The body and the neck are carved from wood. The end of the neck has the form of a horse-head and the sound is not quite like a violin. Legend has it that a Mongol missed his dead horse so much that he used its head, its bones and its hair to build an instrument on which he started to play the familiar noises of his beloved horse.

Legend also has it that a shepherd received a gift from his beloved of a magical horse that could fly. He used it at night to fly to meet her. His jealous wife cut the horse's wings off so that the horse fell from the sky and died. The grieving shepherd made a horse-head fiddle from his beloved horse.

Legend again has it that, after a wicked lord had slaughtered a boy's prized white horse, the horse's spirit came back to Sükhe in a dream and instructed him to make an instrument from the horse's body, so that the two could still be together. Because there is so much love and evil in the world of legend, and because there is so much love and evil in the world, it is right that the family begins to sing near the camel and colt, while the musician concentrates in a centuries-old tradition to bond them. With his instrument he plays polyphonic melodies, since with one stroke of the bow the melody and drone sound at the same time. A miracle! A snow leopard! A wild horse! Art and life come very close here, trusting one another.

The epiphanic moment of the ritual is when the mother camel signals her acceptance of Botok, the rare white camel, by weeping. Here we have our turn-around, and I suppose this is the sentimental moment in the movie that an artist, or a romantic person, should be careful of, but nevertheless one weeps along with the mother. One always does. One is as endangered, as lost, as the world's only truly wild horse, Przewalski's horse, if one does not weep.

Much in the way that we discover we are the weeping camel, we discover the only desert-dwelling bear, the Gobi bear, and at the steppes, hundreds of thousands of gazelles. *Hundreds of thousands of gazelles,* that may be the most wondrous part of being a writer, to write such a phrase and have it be true. Writing rarely, but sometimes, is so easy, like breathing.

Dutch filmmaker Joris Ivens once arrived to film the sound of the Gobi Desert; he can't breathe, he's missing half a lung, he has to be carried, he's nearing ninety. Still, he gets there and back with his documentary, *A Tale of the Wind*. Now, these new directors want the howling, up to ninety miles per hour, to stop. It prevents shooting for nearly half of March. A dry, sandy, and windy world, where just a finger away on a globe are spices, perfumes, grasses, rivers, and oceans. While they wait,

I must complete the long trip on the back of a few thousand vowels and consonants to terraced mud paddies and silt, forgotten algaic moats of summer rice fields. Can I exhume my lover from a visit to the wetlands of China, and beyond? According to legend, choose the right sounds and the one weeping shall cease.

memory of a film, the present, very dark

One becomes visible; therefore, here is a pale green flute now, which Kim brought back as a gift from China. Green marble, weighty, and needing a large room and good wind. I would love to play masterfully, gently, with the wind of the gods, while here are my wind and hands making effort, making low music, breathing. It is quite amazing breathing; it is more amazing breathing into something, from which a sound generously emerges, a low moan, as if one is breathing, although to be honest, I have forgotten, into one's lover's open kiss.

This year, as Mirto, the musical, humming owl said (who is listening, I hope, to a flute in her head and not always to my despair), has been a good bad year. Or a bad good year, I forget, not that it makes much difference, although to her, I suppose there is an enormous difference that I fail to grasp, as important as failing to understand that a saint must never die in a bed of flames.

And yet, a saint dies in a bed of flames. My beloved Rachel died yesterday, and the flute must somehow be played, for Barbara, my friend, who has the same name as dead Rachel's dead daughter, Barbara, dead of breast cancer, who sketches while I play; and for Barbara, the dancer in glass slippers in her chandeliered ballroom. I drum the holes of the flute, stalling for the one present

to be distracted by her red wine a little because I am afraid of the flute, and she needn't hear that. The flute, of course, knows, as a piano knows, that new instruments frighten me. For example, when Kim gave me a black ship of white sails, as

I think of my grand piano, on my fiftieth birthday, to acknowledge the reach of our love into a future in which the black ship of white sails would be paid for, the piano refused to open for me and remained only a black ship. A little later, I saw its white sails in a slight wind, and then in a great wind, and felt better, felt love. *Goodnight*, I should shout, but perhaps I do not want the night to end?

Dear Rachel, your time is very different here now, so you must know that so many younger o'er-flow your funeral hall they spill into the street and are carried off by a stream into deep water.

Listen, especially, as the feeble sound of my lungs from a bad, good, bad year fills the room and beyond, fills the white clouds above the ship sailing west, so that, while the clouds are lined with light as one approaches them, in their own way dazzling, the clouds that one has sailed beyond (and turns back briefly to behold), are blindingly light. And so we know you will only see us that last time. And we may never see you sail on. It is so quiet now without you, without music.

living room, early evening

xxxv

Linda sells the bed, Jacqi takes a table, and Barbara drives me home, Barbara, the old friend, who once got in the middle of the troubles with Kim. Being part Irish and part Scot — and a descendant of the infamous Robert Burns, who had the cocktail of poetry and alcohol ill-measured in his head — Barbara always has held to sexual outlaw status, and introversion, an unusual cocktail in itself. "The troubles" of the Irish, of course, is an understatement, while "the troubles" with me are exaggerated. In other words, there's nothing like seeing an owl awake in the middle of the day to change things around.

Barbara sees an owl from the car in the middle of the day. I find out she's a bit of a birdwatcher. We catch up with one another's stories through Los Angeles, around Palm Springs, and across the desert. Alya's last macrobiotic meal enters our history. The bed at the center of my world no longer exists;

Linda sold it on *craigslist,* after giving up her one day off from 12-hour hospital shifts to cross the Bay Bridge, take photos, post them, and handle the electronic transaction. Everyone deserves a Linda, a mystery who can be trusted. Linda is as here, if there ever was a here, as a peach tree with an owl.

The center is a mirage, but it is also a transaction. Barbara, who was once, and may still be, referred to as the good Chinese lady, accepts a different version of reality every few hours, which makes the owl a compelling symbol, as both the goddess of death and the goddess of wisdom.

The owl, symbolizing a goddess, has the ability to see in the dark and fly noiselessly through the skies. The Queen Mother from the west (often said to be the Gobi Desert) was a fairy goddess with wild hair and supernatural power; and she was a man-eater with a leopard's tail and a tiger's jaw. Also a party girl, she threw feasts high up on a jade tower. When she came from the west to the east, she brought gifts of white jade, white being the symbolic color of the west. Those who are drawn to magic and ancient wisdom, as is the good Chinese lady, will find that these night birds collect around them, proffering their special powers even in daytime.

I am feeling blue (representing the east) in the car when Barbara spots the owl. As is well known, but little understood, owl eyes are fixed, forcing the bird to look straight ahead. However, an owl's neck has fourteen vertebrae, which allows it to turn its head throughout a wide range of motions. Considering perception in a spiritual context, owls represent the true ability to see what is happening around you.

The only owl I've ever seen was sitting on my mailbox around midnight when Jorie and Peter visited us to celebrate my birthday years ago. They were singing when Jorie spotted the Mexican spotted owl. I don't know how Virginia Woolf knew that the beauty of the world was so soon to perish; sad to say, I thought, without understanding, blankly looking away at the time,

the border of 12:00 a.m.– 12:01 a.m.

Maybe sadness begins on one's birth day, a shadow of the goddess of death. I have no idea what to make of it. Certainly, everyone was very moved, each in his or her own way. The singing ceased. It didn't move. We all got very still. For the time being, we became owls. Soon, we went to bed and closed our eyes.

For most people, the owl brings its messages in the night through dreams or meditation. To intuit some life situation, an owl looks upon reality without distortion, or appears to be looking that way, with a fixed gaze and a prehistorically slow, metronomic head, taking it all in. The Mexican spotted owl is an endangered species, like those of us constructing what Frederic Jameson referred to as a depth model of self, profoundly taking it all in.

Seen another way, perhaps the ancient owl is actually quite postmodern, sorting and processing and responding; the fixed gaze, which we anthropomorphically identify with, is a remnant of the depth model, to throw us off the scent, so to speak; the owl's real work is being done with its nose, smelling out prey. The heartfelt gaze, upon which desire preys, is a relic!

But, as Mirto, my owl, says, everyone deserves to be desired. What is to be done? Are we merely prey? A self to be spotted, known, classified, and eventually, endangered? Behind our bewildered gaze is our history of memories and performances. We know our many selves from these memories, and are known by our performances, as in a theater, where those who have given themselves over to the dark awhile gaze upon us.

When we swivel their way, they think they know us by our actions, while they, in turn, are magnified by our attention. They know what shows. And, too, see by their own lights their images reflected, and therefore love, identify, and bond with us. Bondage! The self and the other could finish each other off! Before we know, we are audience and actor.

Let that exchange, recombining, overwhelming, and strange (why so many Barbaras in my life, from the Latin, *the strange, the stranger?*), let art inscribe reality, because, as Mirto proposes, to live with anxiety, reality must be inscribed. Art is made from heady, airy stuff. Once inscribed with ancient magical and spiritual knowledge, poetry may still be the art form most at risk when drawing conclusions; let us leave that to a master actor's lasting impression, or to a master with oil stick, charoal and ink making a single lasting impression on fine linen. Speechless old forms.

Magically, a simple line through a triangle is filled with the presence of matter, of being. The surface of language is picturesque in its way; through the absences in a small and a smaller circle of two letters of love, for example, one may see to infinity.

If art is open to interpretation, how much more careful must the word be, because of its history as a messenger of the imagination but, more practically, of the marketplace, the hearth, the boudoir, and other distinguished and not so distinguished locations. Words participate in all manner of charity, obscenity, cruelty, serendipity, war, and so on. Made of itself, language has made of itself a necessity, in other words.

Truth be told, we are looking at them together now, strangers, friends, as they materialize Osip Mandelstam's *necklace of dead bees* — there is love, a fragile line composed of death. The imagination does wonders for words,

as a bee traveling from blossom to blossom for nectar to make honey transfers pollen from plant to plant, fertilizing them to bear blackberries, cherries, avocados, watermelon, sunflowers, almonds, apples, and more. There are many martyrs when one encounters language at her repast; strangely, fortunately, poetry changes.

Now I am at home writing a book that changes. In it, my mother and I no longer need medication to manage our affairs, and my brother returns his wristwatch to the Dalai Lama, because, as Mirto says, entitlement is a disagreement with reality. My Greek friend Olga appears to present a small Buddha to Kim, who gratefully acknowledges its beauty and importance. Olga replies, "Think nothing of it."

Tucson, high noon

Finally, here is a little *rembetika,* the music of the Greek underground that Olga brings with her. It originated in the hashish dens of Piraeus and Thessaloniki around the turn of the twentieth century. Greeks forced out of Asia Minor, hanging out, unemployed, hiding out, would chip off resin from compressed blocks of "little hairs" collected from Cannabis plants and get stoned. Insects adhering to the little hairs die or, as it is said, "lose time."

These Greek composers live on; they lose time by choice, in a solo bouzouki, sometimes accompanied by baglama and percussion. They make Greek popular music around the early 1950s, during the Junta, when certain things could not be said out loud (*else death or lost time*), but could be disguised in song. The song *Elsa Se Fovame* (*Elsa You Scare Me*) is not about trouble with a woman; *E.L.S.A.* refers to the *Elliniki Stratiotiki Astynomia,* the military police that tortured anybody suspected by the Junta of being a dissenter. Olga's father Nicholas, himself a colonel in the Junta, nevertheless was picked up by them, under cover of darkness, as the cliché of subversion had it (a very dark time

around 2 a.m., suburb of Athens

in the mind of a young poet in her bed in a nightshirt, *under cover of darkness*),… but that is another story. Let us rather stay with the song.

No sooner do lovers meet, they rummage around, they hear music, and ask for

94

and receive the best room. No sooner do they settle in, they are in church, but the church has vanished. Lovers prefer it, hung with one of the famous mirrors of legend, where things seem not as they are but, magically, become what they seem, the windfall from the field of quicksilver. I wish I could sing about, or at least write better about love, rather than simply empty my suitcase.

Whoever loves lives through a fretted night with a telescope, never mind who is holding it. The world of objects and places and colors, numbers and fragments, is shaken free as if a wind has loosened ripe grapes from an old vineyard. Do you hear them come loose? Good night.

Then you must leave, taking me with you? Now that you might know who I am, or was, Jane, *who are you?*

Napa, 11:11 p.m.

NOTES

Paragraph breaks added, commas added, and some repetition deleted in an otherwise direct quotation from SPECIAL EDITION, *La Voz de Aztlan*, "US/Mexico Border Crisis," Hector Carreon, Los Angeles, California, June 5, 2000.

Hexagram #3, "Difficulty at the Beginning," *I Ching or Book of Changes*, 3rd. ed., Bollingen Series XIX, Richard Wilhelm and Cary F. Baynes tr. (Princeton NJ: Princeton University Press, 1967, 1st ed. 1950).

The "implications of the title," *Critique of I Ching* and *Commentary on I Ching*, Eastern Han Dynasty, Zheng Xuan.

Anne Carson, translating Paul Celan, "Sprach Auch Du," *Economy of the Unlost: Reading Simonides of Keos with Paul Celan* (Princeton, NJ: Princeton University Press, 1999).

Anne Carson, *...the little raw soul...* from "The Glass Essay," *Glass, Irony, and God* (New Directions Publishing Corporation, 1995).

"Schlafenzange" ("Temple-pincers"), Paul Celan, *Atemwende*, 1967. See John Felstiner, note on shock therapy, tr., *Selected Poems and Prose of Paul Celan* (W.W. Norton, 2000).

John Felstiner, quoting lines from Celan's Bremen speech, *Paul Celan: Poet, Survivor, Jew* (New Haven: Yale University Press, 1997).

"Die Ewigkeiten" ("The Eternities"), Paul Celan, translated by Pierre Joris, *Lightduress* (Green Integer, 2005).

The three water poems are inspired by poems by Brian Russell.

"Woman found dead in Okura Hotel," *Amsterdam News*, June 11, 2006.

" 'American Beauties': Images of Softness Rendered in Concrete," on Louise Bourgeois, Michael Brenson, *New York Times*, March 15, 1991.

Summary of the film *The Story of the Weeping Camel* pieced together from various press releases from its distributor, National Geographic World Films.

Splendid with ill-fortune

— Ugo Foscolo

Also Available from saturnalia books:

FAMOUS LAST WORDS by Catherine Pierce
WINNER OF THE SATURNALIA BOOKS POETRY PRIZE 2007

DUMMY FIRE by Sarah Vap
WINNER OF THE SATURNALIA BOOKS POETRY PRIZE 2006

CORRESPONDENCE by Kathleen Graber
WINNER OF THE SATURNALIA BOOKS POETRY PRIZE 2005

THE BABIES by Sabrina Orah Mark
WINNER OF THE SATURNALIA BOOKS POETRY PRIZE 2004

STIGMATA ERRATA ETCETERA
Poems by Bill Knott / Artwork by Star Black
ARTIST/POET COLLABORATION SERIES NUMBER THREE

ING GRISH
Poems by John Yau / Artwork by Thomas Nozkowski
ARTIST/POET COLLABORATION SERIES NUMBER TWO

BLACKBOARDS
Poems by Tomaž Šalamun / Artwork by Metka Krašovec
ARTIST/POET COLLABORATION SERIES NUMBER ONE

In Cooperation with Fence Books:

Apprehend by Elizabeth Robinson
Father of Noise by Anthony McCann
Nota by Martin Corless-Smith
The Red Bird by Joyelle McSweeney
Can You Relax in My House by Michael Earl Craig

Midnights is the fourth of a series of collaborations between artists and poets for
saturnalia books.
Midnights was printed using the font New Baskerville.

www.saturnaliabooks.com